THE POPULAR HITS
COLLECTION

ARRANGED BY RICHARD BRADLEY

Richard Bradley is one of the world's best-known and best-selling arrangers of piano music for print. His success can be attributed to years of experience as a teacher and his understanding of students' and players' needs. His innovative piano methods for adults (*Bradley's How to Play Piano* – Adult Books 1, 2, and 3) and kids (*Bradley for Kids* – Red, Blue, and Green Series) not only teach the instrument, but they also teach musicianship each step of the way.

Originally from the Chicago area, Richard completed his undergraduate and graduate work at the Chicago Conservatory of Music and Roosevelt University. After college, Richard became a print arranger for Hansen Publications and later became music director of Columbia Pictures Publications. In 1977, he co-founded his own publishing company, Bradley Publications, which is now exclusively distributed worldwide by Warner Bros. Publications.

Richard is equally well known for his piano workshops, clinics, and teacher training seminars. He was a panelist for the first and second Keyboard Teachers' National Video Conferences, which were attended by more than 20,000 piano teachers throughout the United States.

The home video version of his adult teaching method, *How to Play Piano With Richard Bradley*, was nominated for an American Video Award as Best Music Instruction Video, and, with sales climbing each year since its release, it has brought thousands of adults to—or back to—piano lessons. Still, Richard advises, "The video can only get an adult started and show them what they can do. As they advance, all students need direct input from an accomplished teacher."

Additional Richard Bradley videos aimed at other than the beginning pianist include *How to Play Blues Piano* and *How to Play Jazz Piano*. As a frequent television talk show guest on the subject of music education, Richard's many appearances include "Hour Magazine" with Gary Collins, "The Today Show," and "Mother's Day" with former "Good Morning America" host Joan Lunden, as well as dozens of local shows.

Project Manager: Zobeida Pérez
Art Design: Carmen Fortunato

BRADLEY™ is a trademark of Warner Bros. Publications

Bradley
Publications
a division of
RBR Communications, Inc.

CONTENTS

More Than That

Recorded by Backstreet Boys

Words and Music by
FRANCIZ & LePONT and ADAM ANDERS
Arranged by Richard Bradley

4

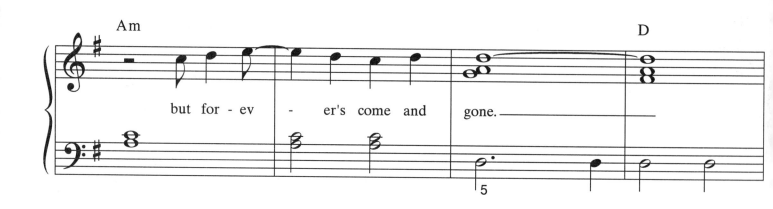

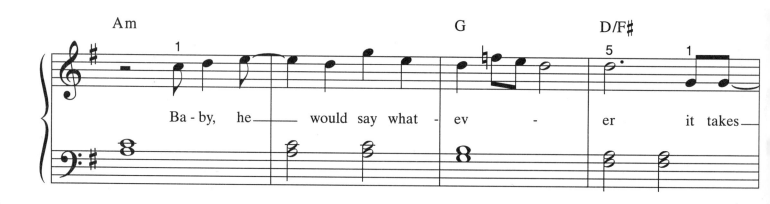

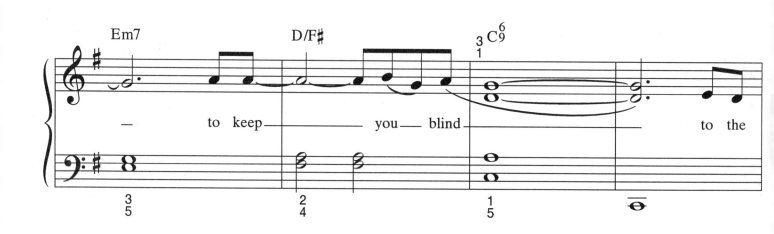

6

Verse 3:
Baby, you deserve much better.
What's the use in holding on?
Don't you see it's now or never?
'Cause I just can't be friends,
Baby, knowing in the end,
That I will love you more than that.

Gone

Recorded by ★NSYNC

Words and Music by
JUSTIN TIMBERLAKE
and WADE J. ROBSON
Arranged by Richard Bradley

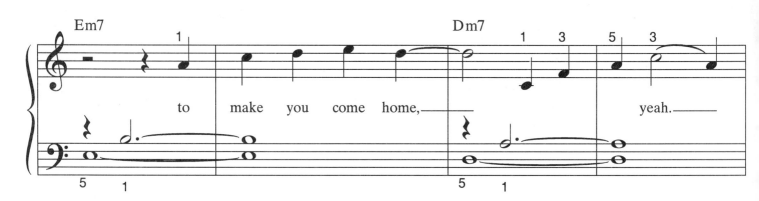

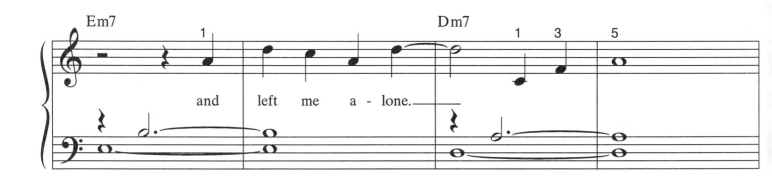

Gone - 8 - 1

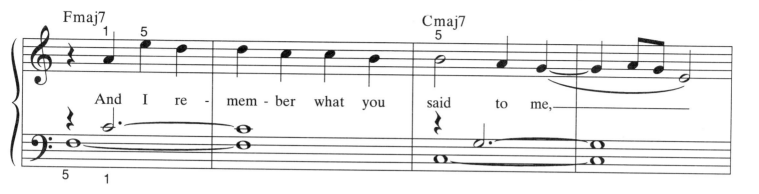

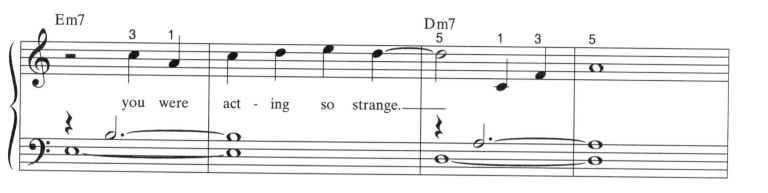

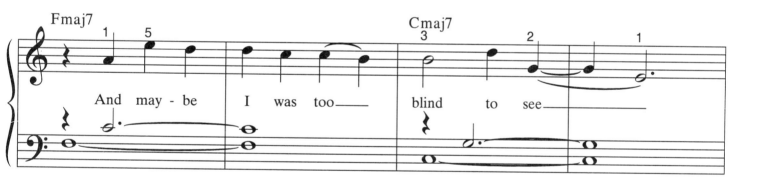

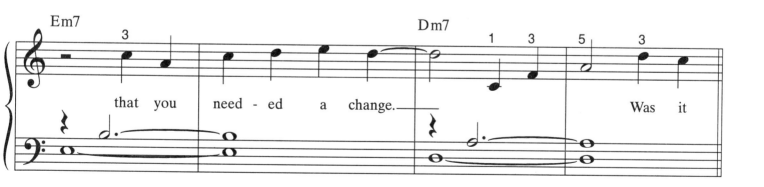

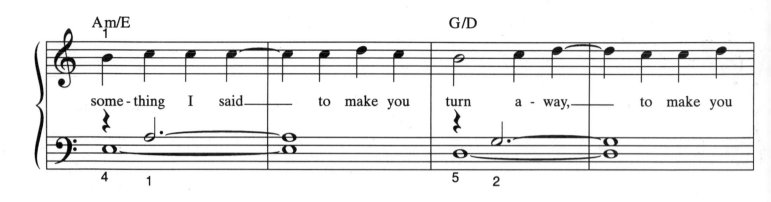

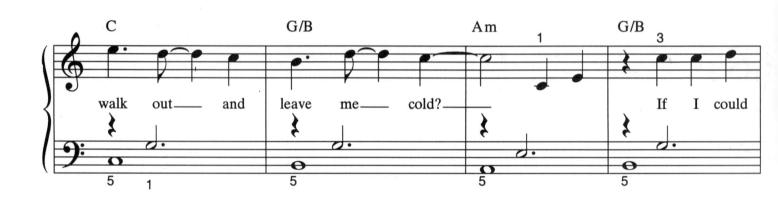

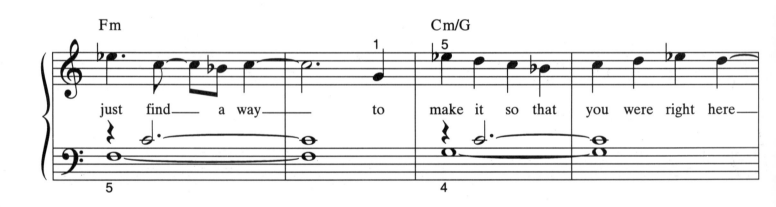

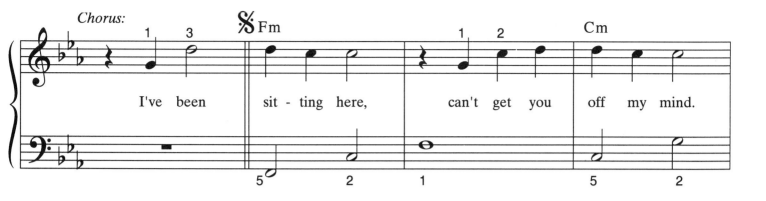

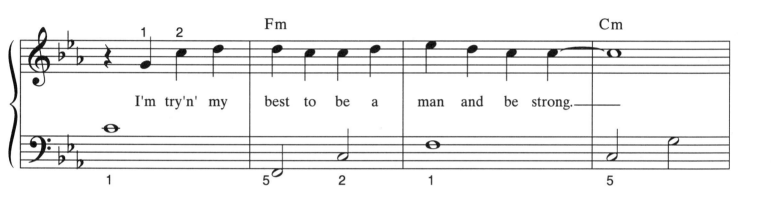

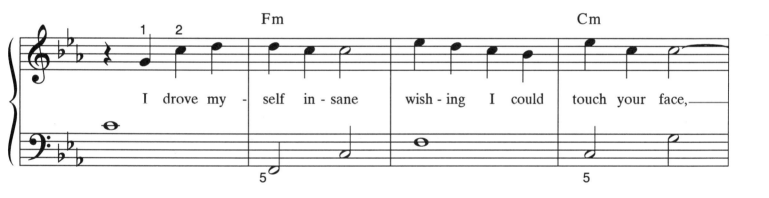

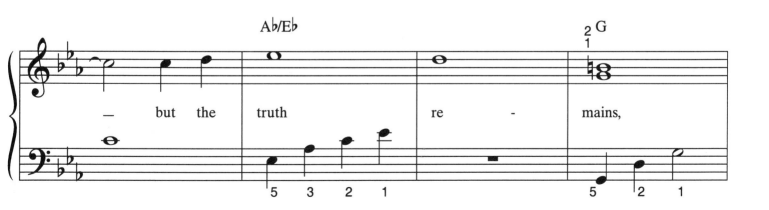

12

14

Cm
B♭/D
we are a - part, am I
Fm
Cm
still in your heart? Ba - by,
B♭
Cm
why don't you see that I
F
G
need you here with me?
D.S. 𝄋 al Coda 𝄌
Oh. I've been

Coda

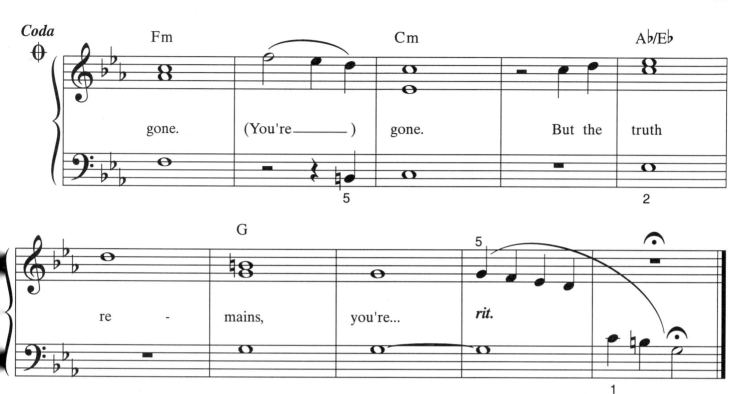

Fm

gone.

(You're———)

Cm

gone.

But the truth

A♭/E♭

G

re - mains,

you're...

rit.

Verse 2:
Now, I don't wanna make excuses, baby.
Won't change the fact that you're gone.
But if there's something that I could do,
Won't you please let me know?
The time is passing so slowly now,
Guess that's my life without you.
And maybe I could change my everyday,
But, baby, I don't want to.
So I'll just hang around and find some things to do
To take my mind off missing you.
And I know in my heart,
You can't say that you don't love me too.
Please say you do, yeah.
(To Chorus:)

I'm Like a Bird

Recorded by Nelly Furtado

Words and Music by
NELLY FURTADO
Arranged by Richard Bradley

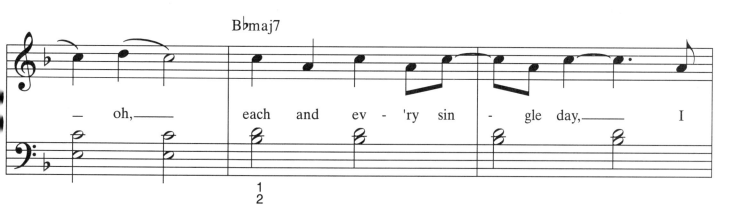

I'm Like a Bird - 6 - 4

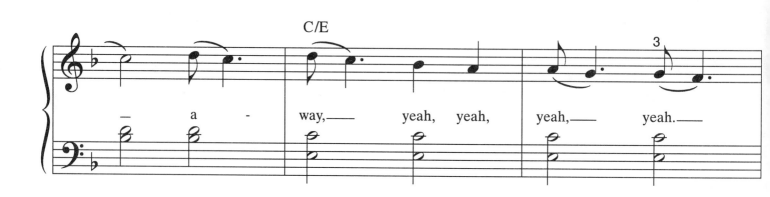

Verse 2:
Your faith in me brings me to tears
Even after all these years.
And it pains me so much
To tell that you don't know me that well.
And tho' my love is rare, yeah,
And tho' my love is true.
(To Chorus:)

Thank You

Recorded by Dido

Words and Music by
DIDO ARMSTRONG
and PAUL HERMAN
Arranged by Richard Bradley

1. My tea's gone cold, I'm won-d'ring why I got out of bed at
2. *See additional lyrics*

all. The morn - ing rain clouds up my win - dow and

I can't see at all. And e - ven if I could, it - 'd

Thank You - 4 - 1

23

all be grey, but your pic - ture on —— my —— wall, it re -

minds me that it's not so bad,—— it's not so bad.——

not so bad,—— it's not so bad.—— And I—— want to

Thank You - 4 - 2

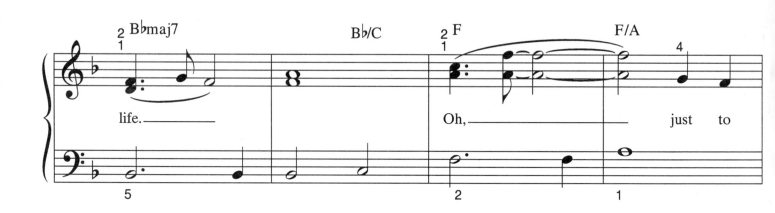

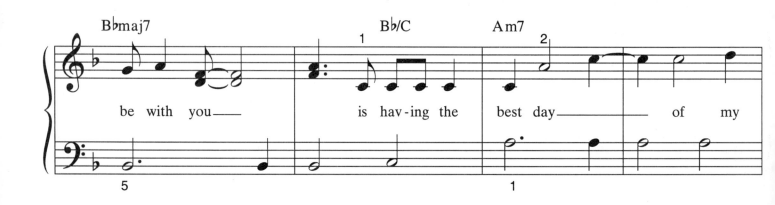

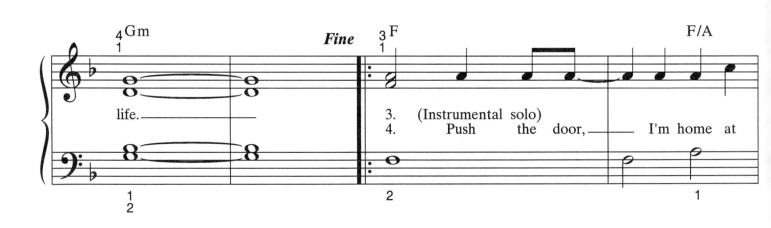

Verse 2:
I drank too much last night, got bills to pay,
My head just feels in pain.
I missed the bus and there'll be hell today,
I'm late for work again.
And even if I'm there, they'll all imply
That I might not last the day.
And then you call me and it's not so bad, it's not so bad.
(To Chorus:)

All or Nothing

Recorded by O-Town

Words and Music by
WAYNE ANTHONY HECTOR
and STEVE MAC
Arranged by Richard Bradley

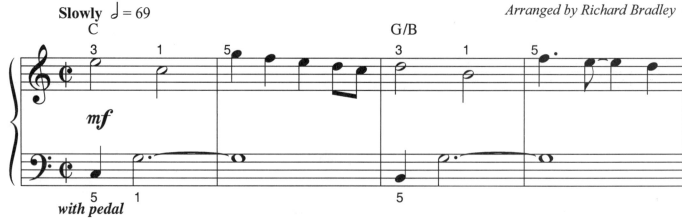

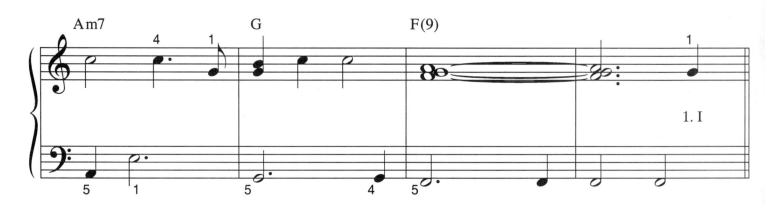

know when he's been on your mind,___ that dis - tant look is

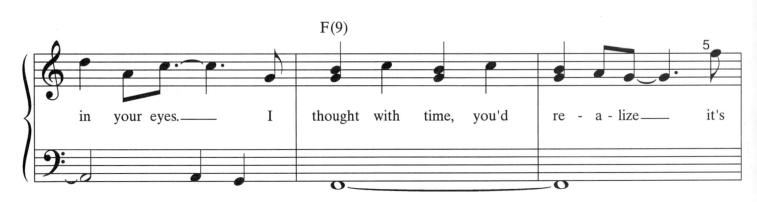

in your eyes.___ I thought with time, you'd re - a - lize___ it's

All or Nothing - 7 - 1

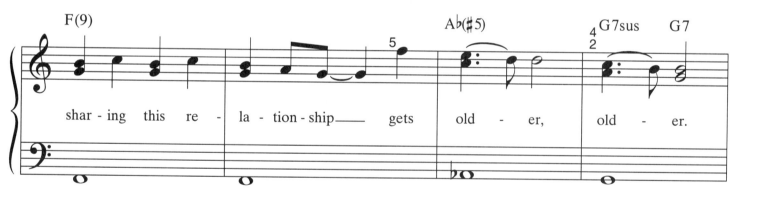

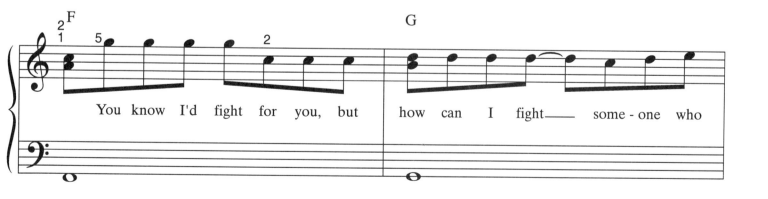

28

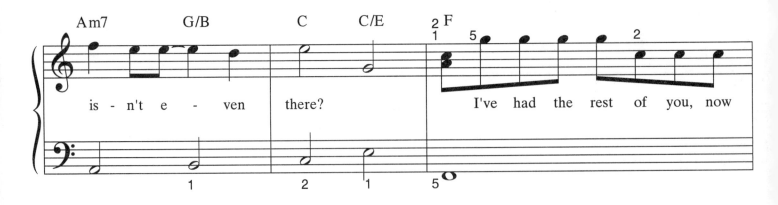

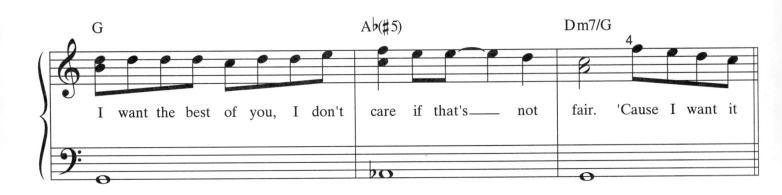

Chorus:

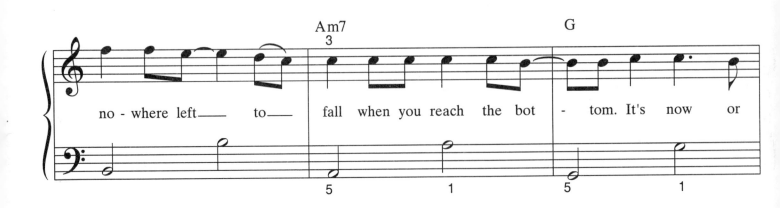

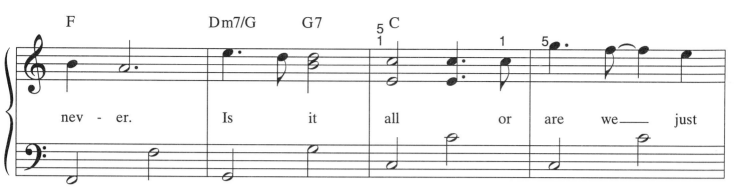

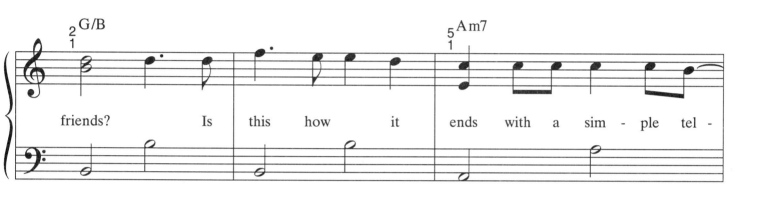

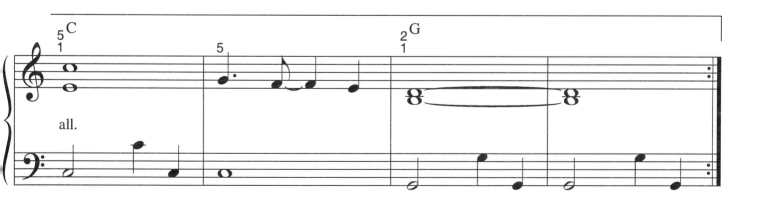

30

All or Nothing - 7 - 5

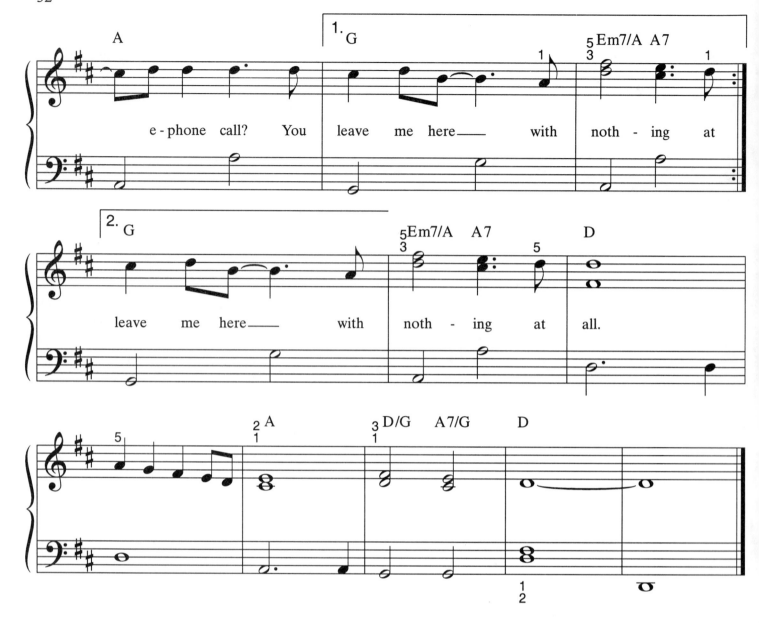

Verse 2:
There are times, it seems to me,
I'm sharing you in memories.
I feel it in my heart but I don't show it, show it.
And then there's times you look at me
As though I'm all that you can see.
Those times I don't believe it's right. I know it, know it.
Don't make me promises.
Baby, you never did know how to keep them well.
I've had the rest of you, now I want the best of you.
It's time to show and tell.
'Cause I want it...
(To Chorus:)

When It's Over

Recorded by Sugar Ray

Words and Music by
MARK McGRATH, STAN FRAZIER, RODNEY SHEPPARD
CRAIG BULLOCK and MATHEW KARGES
Arranged by Richard Bradley

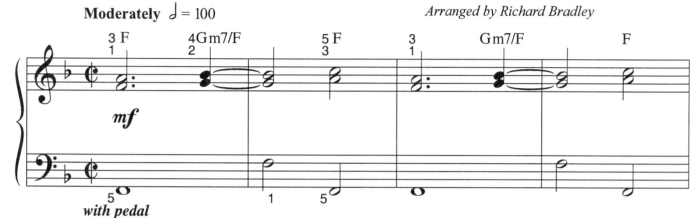

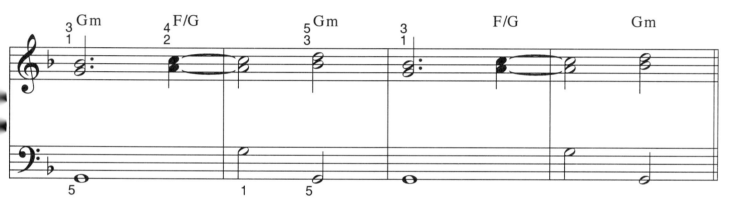

1. When it's o - ver, that's the time I fall in

love a - gain.

When It's Over - 7 - 1

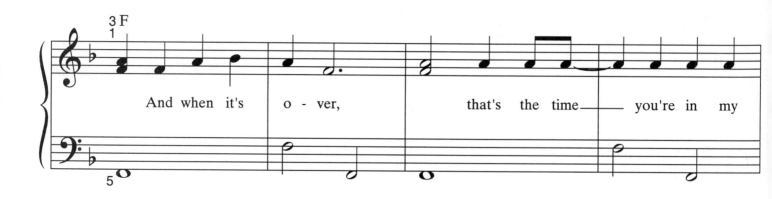

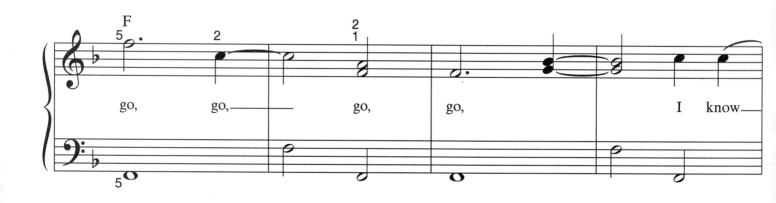

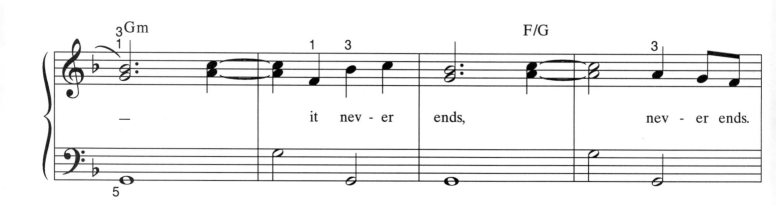

Chorus:

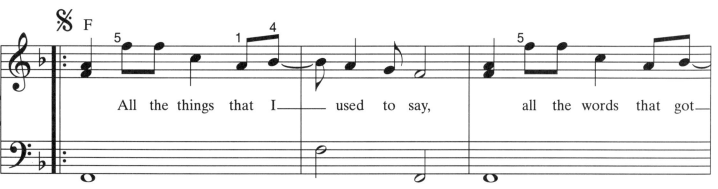

All the things that I—— used to say, all the words that got——

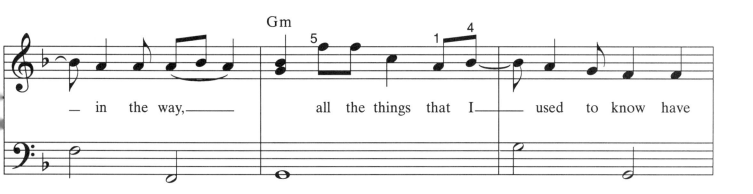

—— in the way,———— all the things that I—— used to know have

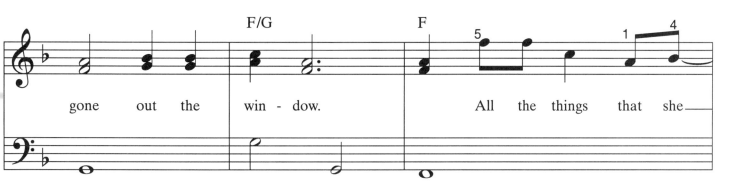

gone out the win - dow. All the things that she——

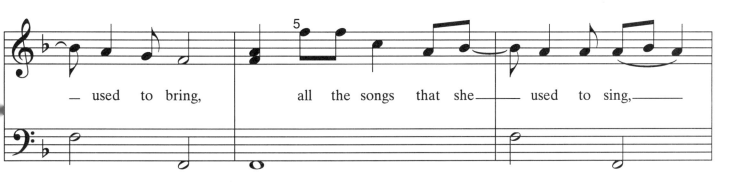

—— used to bring, all the songs that she—— used to sing,————

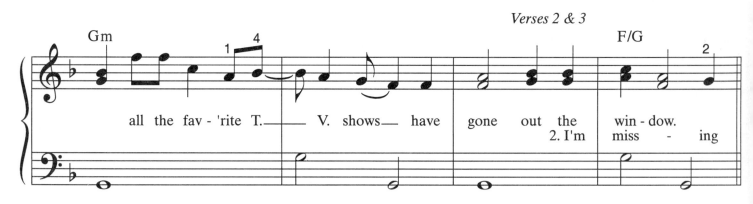

all the fav - 'rite T._____ V. shows___ have gone out the win - dow.
2. I'm miss - ing

you. I nev - er knew_____ how much she

loved me. I'm miss - ing

you.___ I nev - er knew_____ how much you

38

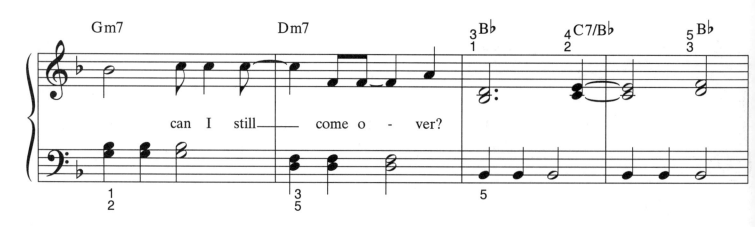

can I still —— come o - ver?

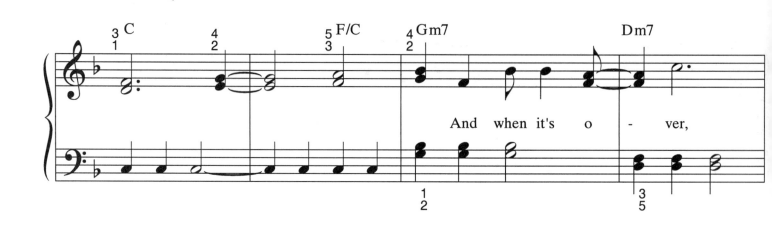

And when it's o - ver,

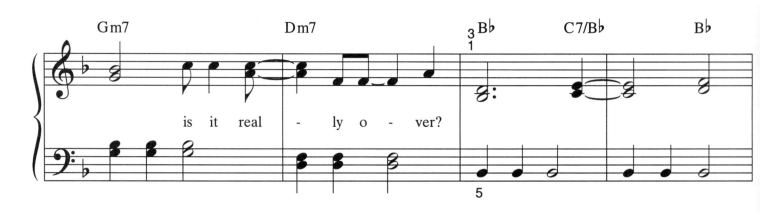

is it real - ly o - ver?

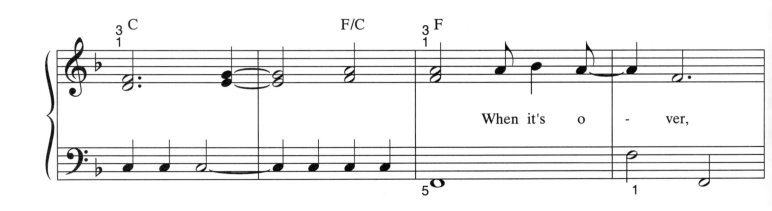

When it's o - ver,

that's   the   time___   I   fall   in   love   a - gain.___

D.S. % *and fade*

Verse 3:
I'm wishing you,
You never said you were pretending.
I'm wishing you,
You'd feel the same and just come back to me.
I need you.
And when you go, go, go, go,
I know it never ends, never ends.

There You'll Be

From Touchstone Pictures' *Pearl Harbor*
Recorded by Faith Hill

Words and Music by
DIANE WARREN
Arranged by Richard Bradley

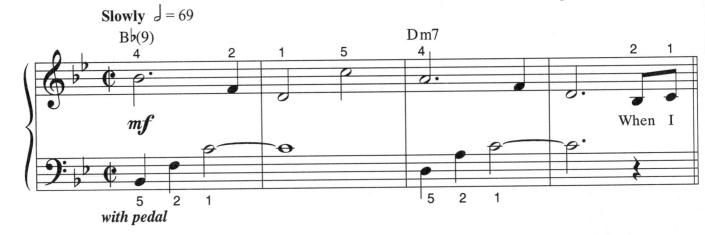

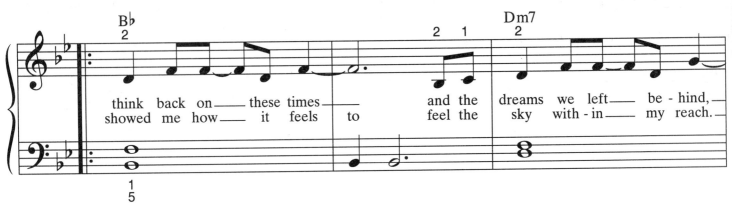

There You'll Be - 6 - 1

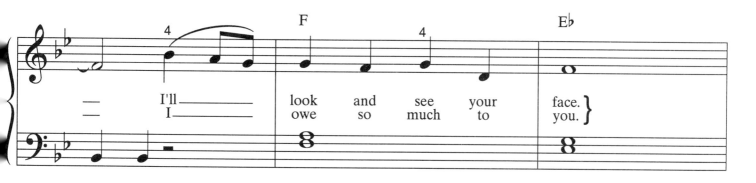

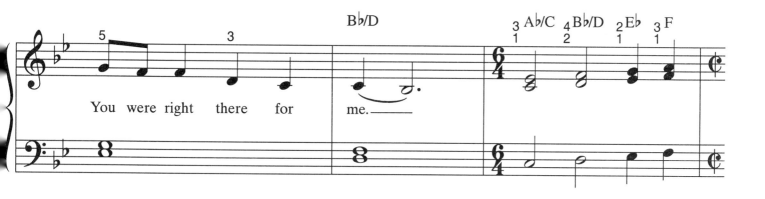

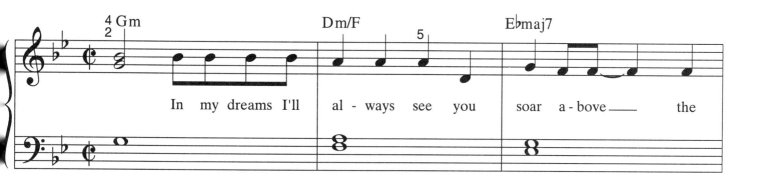

There You'll Be - 6 - 2

42

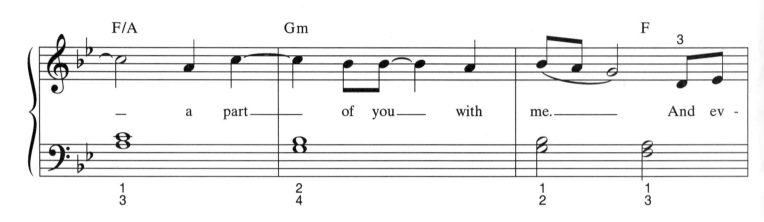

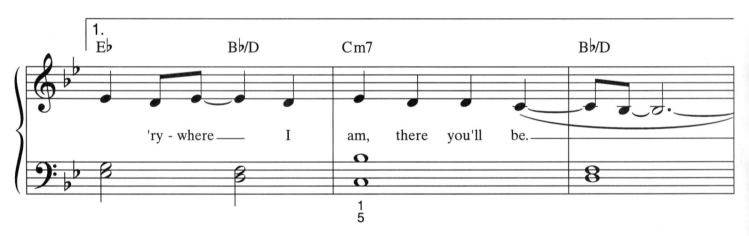

There You'll Be - 6 - 3

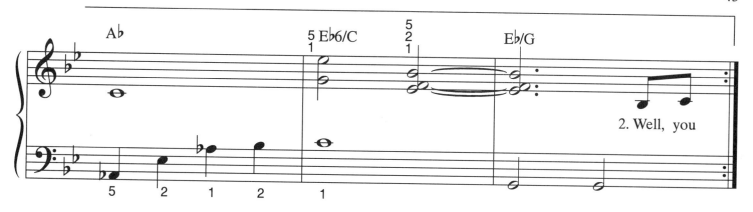

There You'll Be - 6 - 4

44

Nobody Wants to Be Lonely

Recorded by Ricky Martin with Christina Aguilera

Words and Music by
DESMOND CHILD, VICTORIA SHAW
and GARY BURR
Arranged by Richard Bradley

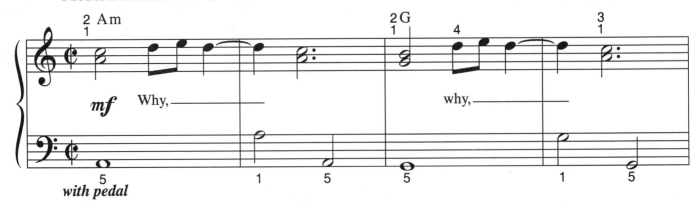

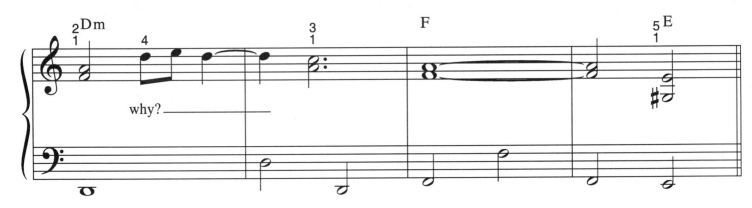

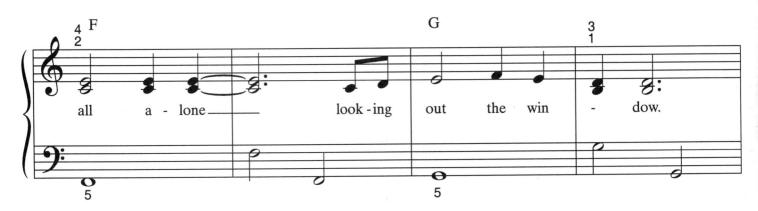

Nobody Wants to Be Lonely - 6 - 1

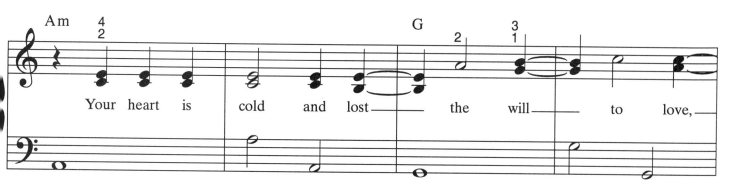

Your heart is cold and lost____ the will____ to love,____

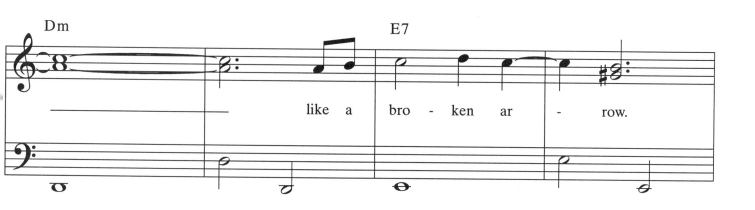

____ like a bro - ken ar - row.

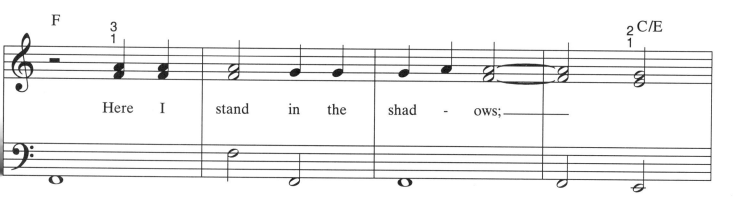

Here I stand in the shad - ows;____

come to me, come to me, can't you see that...

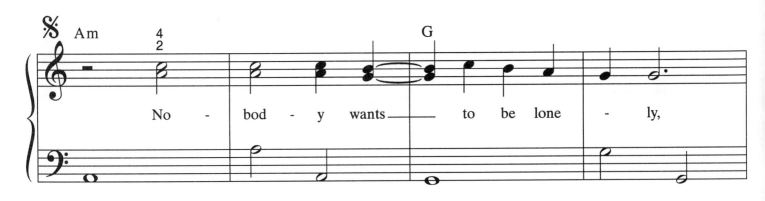

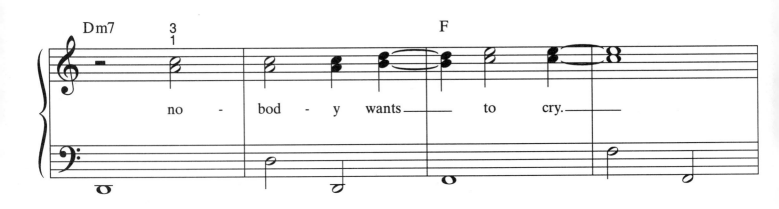

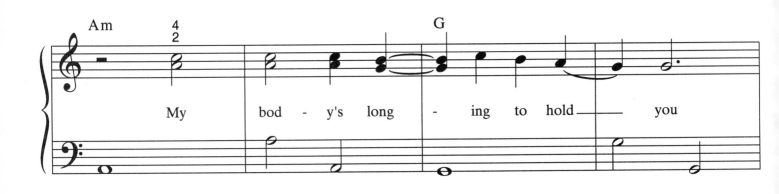

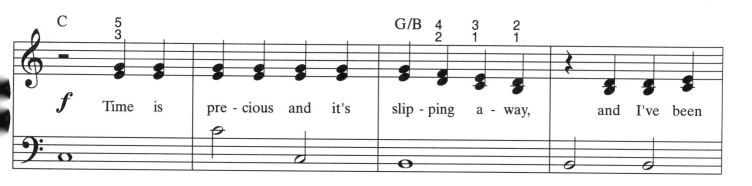

50

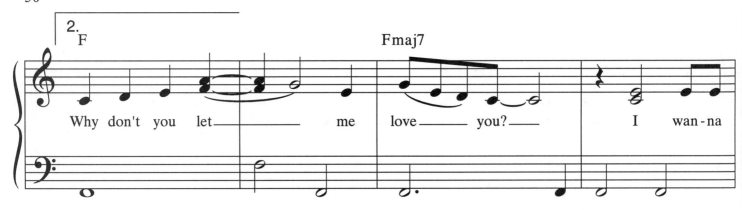

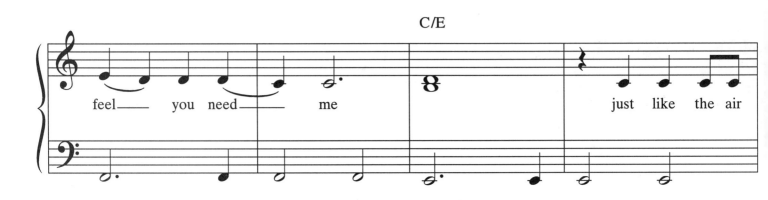

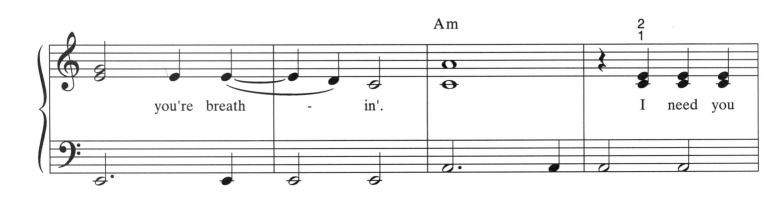

walk - a - way, don't walk a - way, no, no, no... No -

bod - y wants to be lone - ly, no -

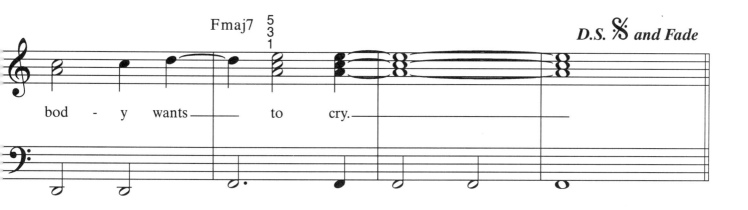

bod - y wants to cry.

D.S. 𝄋 and Fade

Verse 2:
Can you hear my voice?
Do you hear my song?
It's a serenade
So your heart can find me.
And suddenly you're flying down the stairs
Into my arms, baby.
Before I start going crazy,
Run to me, run to me
'Cause I'm dyin'.
(To Chorus:)

I Hope You Dance

Recorded by Lee Ann Womack with Sons of the Desert

Words and Music by
MARK D. SANDERS
and TIA SILLERS
Arranged by Richard Bradley

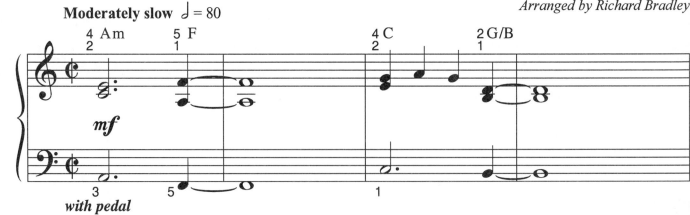

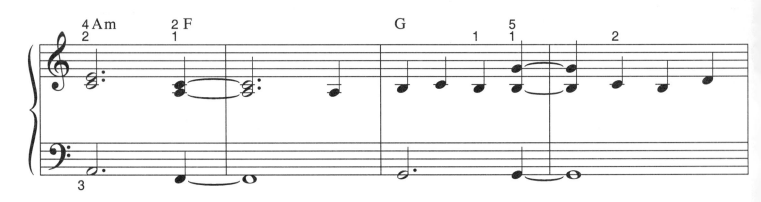

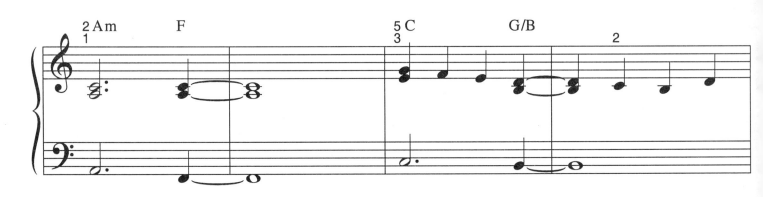

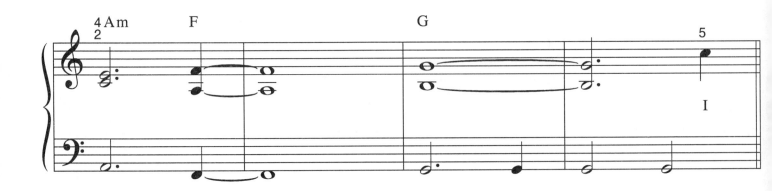

I Hope You Dance - 5 - 1

Verse:

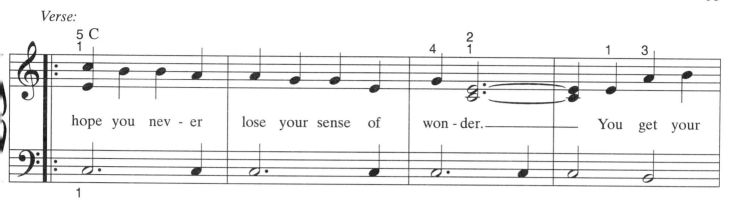

hope you nev - er lose your sense of won - der._____ You get your

fill to eat, but al - ways keep that hun - ger._____ May you

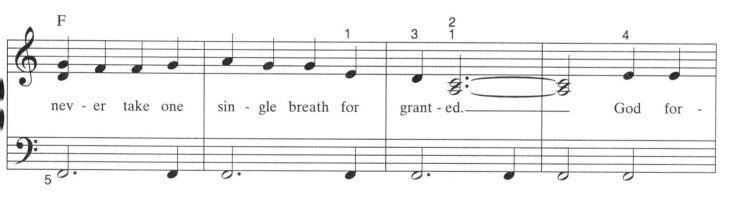

nev - er take one sin - gle breath for grant - ed._____ God for -

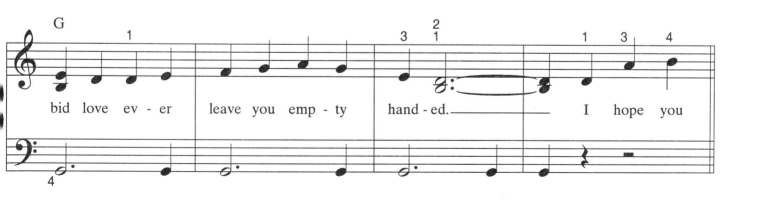

bid love ev - er leave you emp - ty hand - ed._____ I hope you

Chorus:

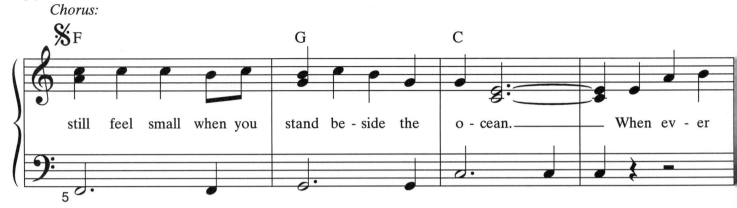

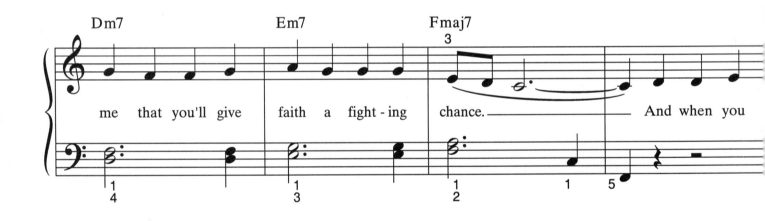

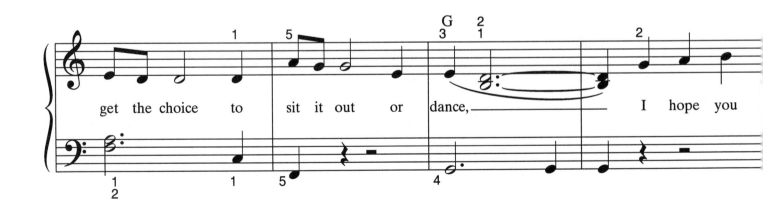

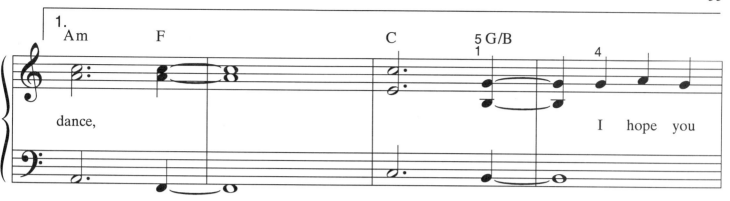

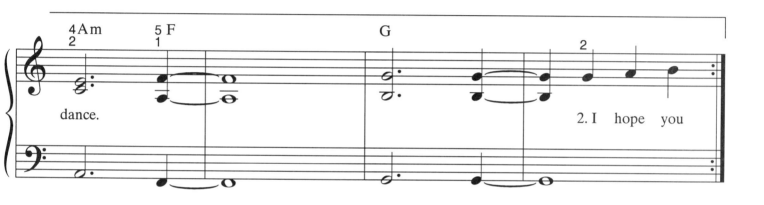

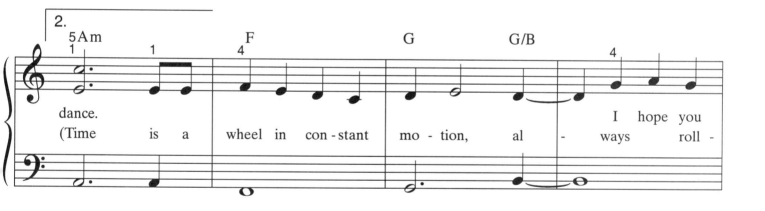

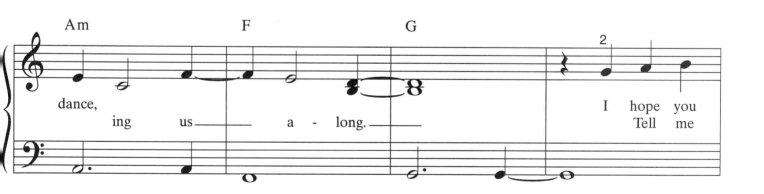

56

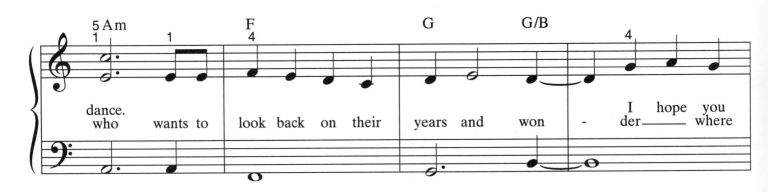

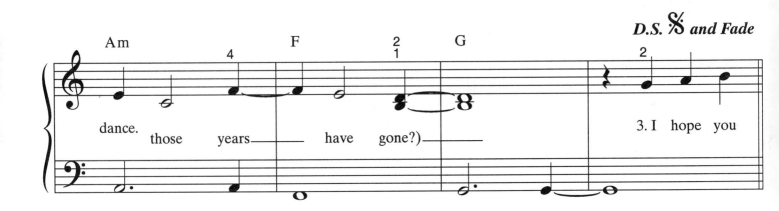

D.S. 𝄋 *and Fade*

Verse 2:

I hope you never fear those mountains in the distance,
Never settle for the path of least resistance.
Livin' might mean takin' chances but they're worth takin'.
Lovin' might be a mistake but it's worth makin'.

Chorus 2:

Don't let some hell-bent heart leave you bitter.
When you come close to sellin' out, reconsider.
Give the heavens above more than just a passing glance,
And when you get the chance to sit it out or dance,...

Breathe

Recorded by Faith Hill

Words and Music by
STEPHANIE BENTLEY
and HOLLY LAMAR
Arranged by Richard Bradley

Breathe - 5 - 1

58

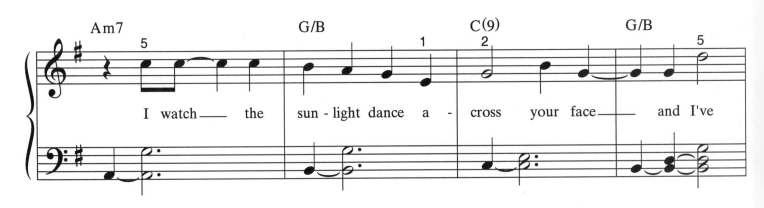

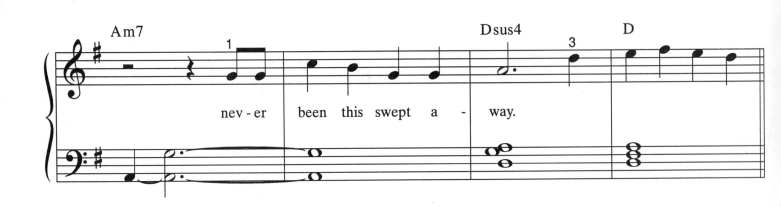

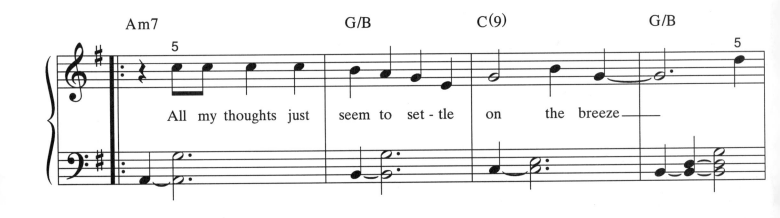

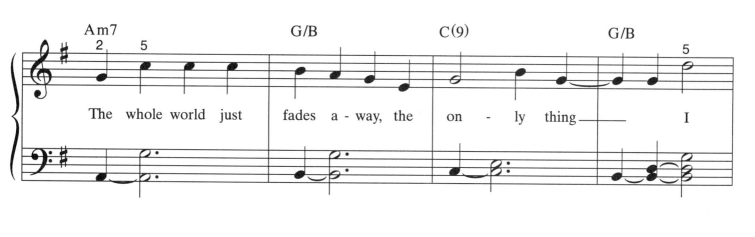

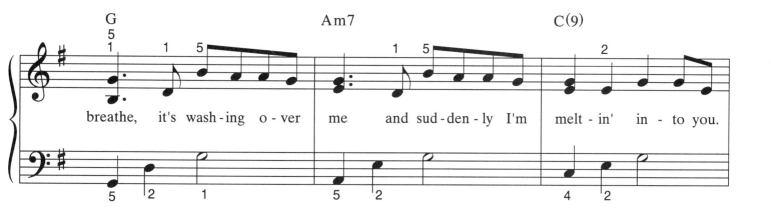

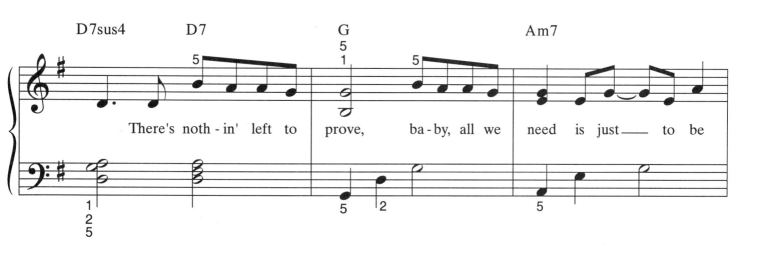

caught up in the touch, the slow and stead - y

rush. And ba - by, is - n't that the way____ that love's sup - posed

to be?

I can feel you

breathe.____ Just

breathe.

To Coda ⊕

Verse 2:
In a way, I know my heart is waking up
As all the walls come tumblin' down.
Closer than I've ever felt before
And I know and you know
There's no need for words right now.

Breathe - 5 - 5

This I Promise You

Recorded by ★NSYNC

Words and Music by
RICHARD MARX
Arranged by Richard Bradley

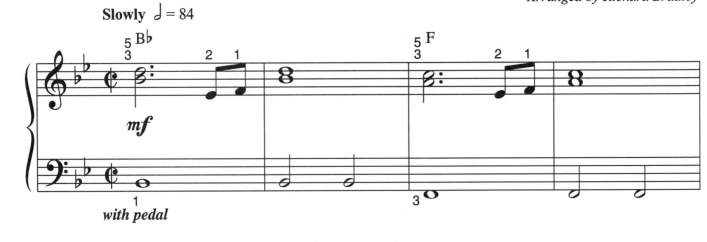

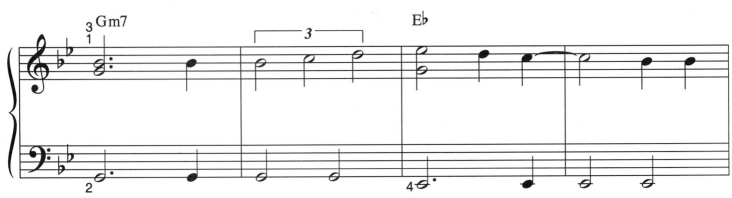

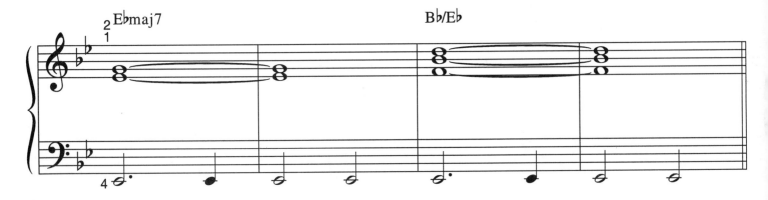

This I Promise You - 6 - 1

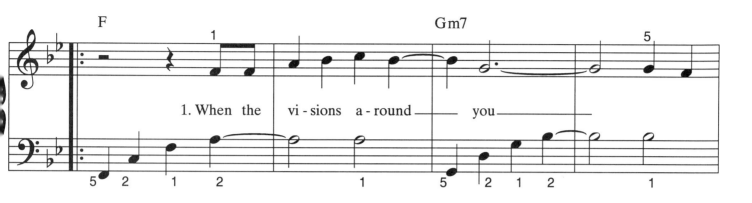

1. When the vi-sions a-round you

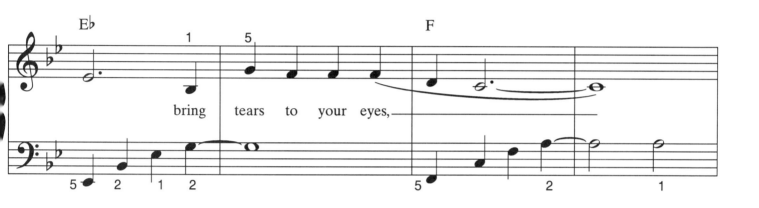

bring tears to your eyes,

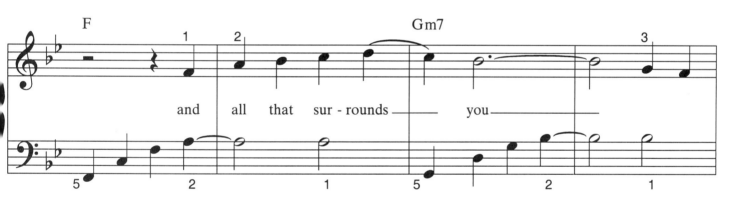

and all that sur-rounds you

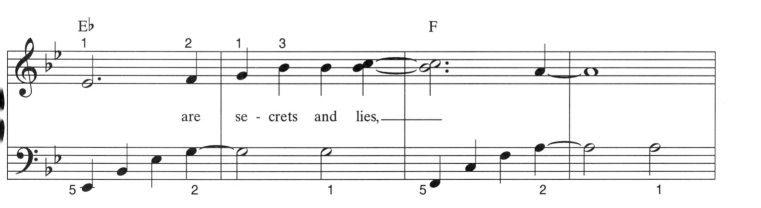

are se-crets and lies,

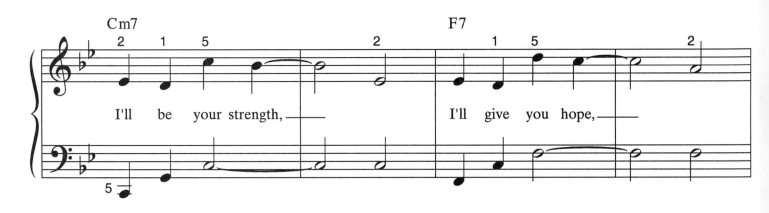

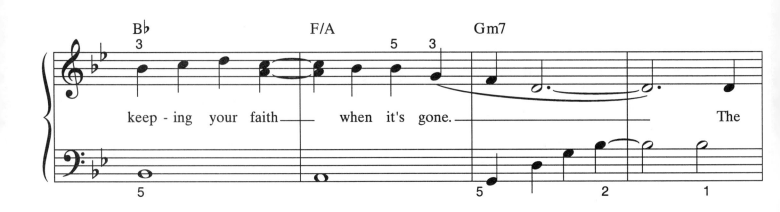

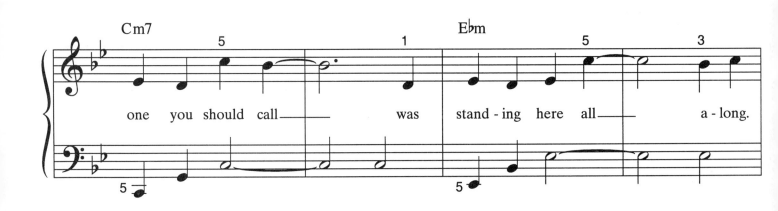

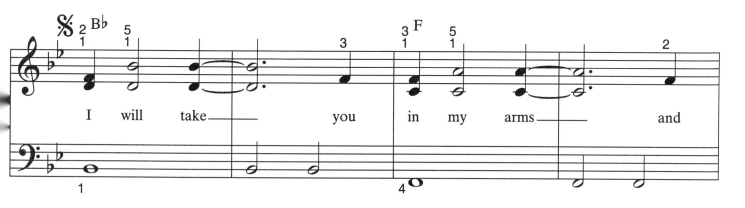

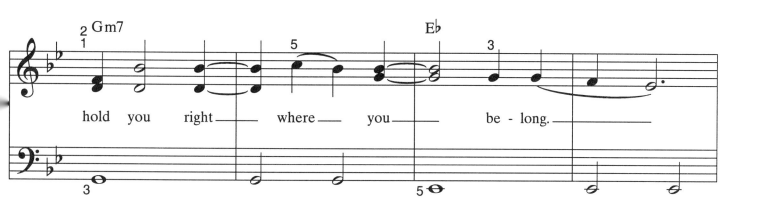

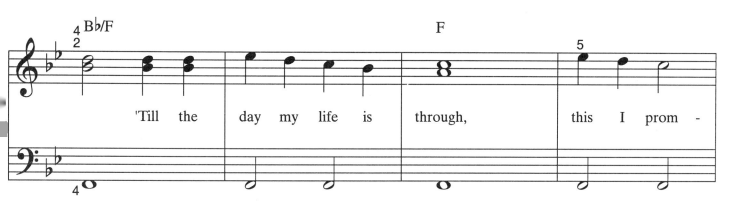

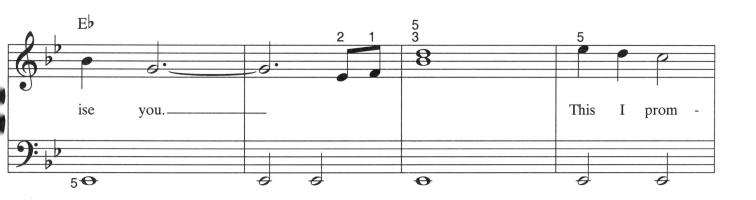

66

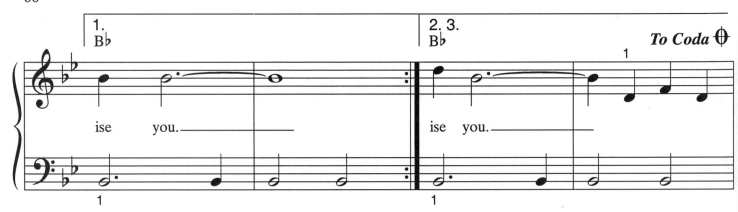

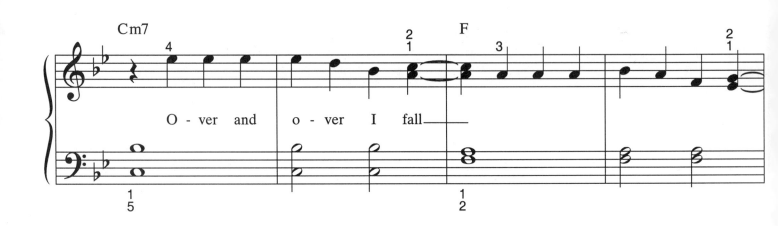

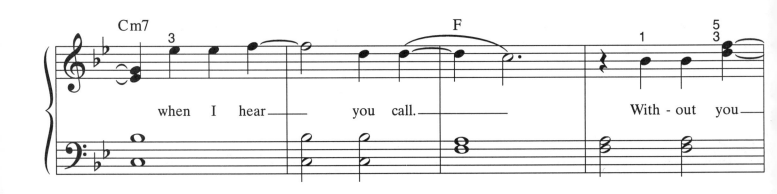

This I Promise You - 6 - 5

Coda

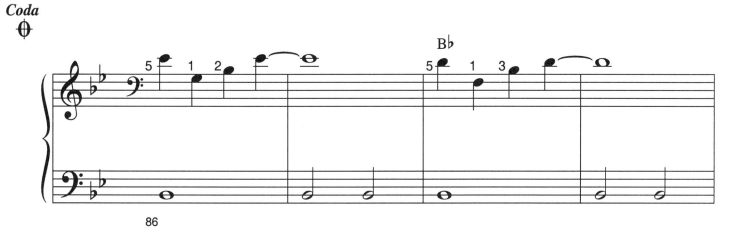

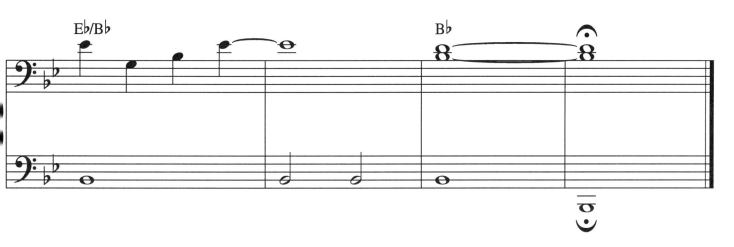

Verse 2:
I've loved you forever in life times before.
And I promise you, never will you hurt anymore.
I give you my word. I give you my heart.
This is the battle I've won.
And with this vow, forever has now begun.
Just close your eyes each loving day
And know this feeling won't go away.

1st time : 'Till the day my life is through,
This I promise you, this I promise you.

2nd time : Every word I say is true,
This I promise you. Ooh, I promise you.

Show Me the Meaning of Being Lonely

Recorded by Backstreet Boys

Words and Music by
MAX MARTIN and HERBERT CRICHLOW
Arranged by Richard Bradley

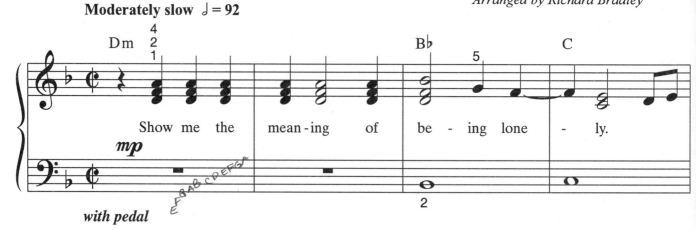

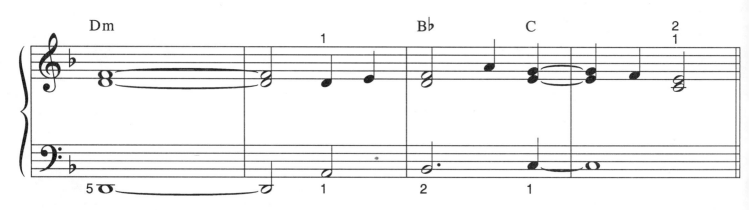

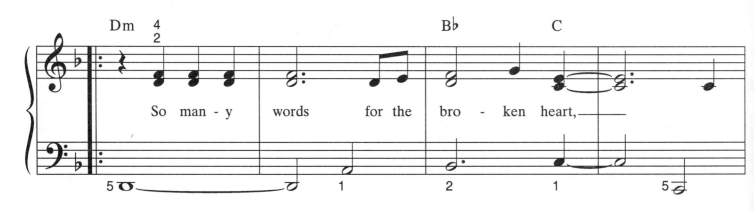

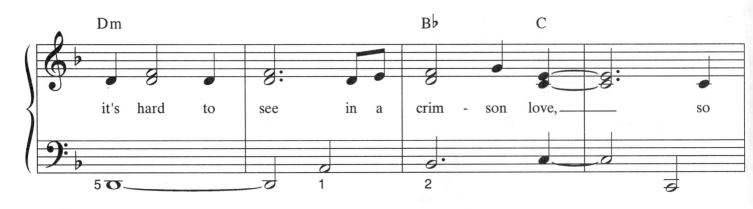

Show Me the Meaning of Being Lonely - 6 - 1

70

Show Me the Meaning of Being Lonely - 6 - 4

72

Verse 2:
Life goes on as it never ends.
Eyes of stone observe the trends,
They never say, forever gaze.
If only guilty roads to an endless love,
There's no control.
Are you with me now?
Your every wish will be done, they tell me . . .

What a Girl Wants

Recorded by Christina Aguilera

Words and Music by
GUY ROCHE and SHELLY PEIKEN
Arranged by Richard Bradley

Slow, funky groove ♩ = 72

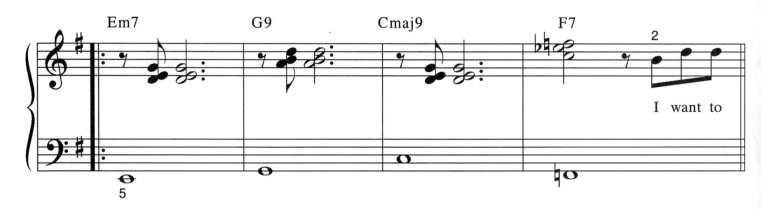

What a Girl Wants - 5 - 1

thank you for giv-ing me time to breathe. Like a rock you wait -

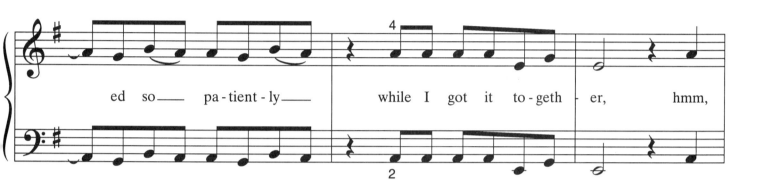

ed so pa-tient-ly while I got it to-geth - er, hmm,

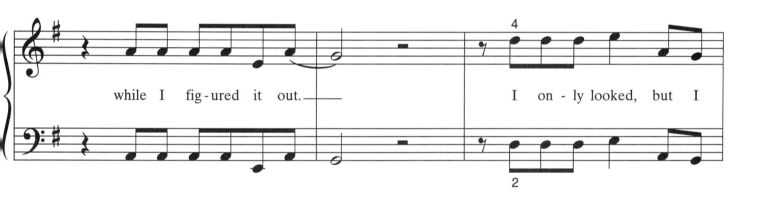

while I fig-ured it out. I on - ly looked, but I

nev - er touched 'cause in my heart was a pic-ture of us

Verse 2:
A weaker man might have walked away, but you had faith,
Strong enough to move over and give me space
While I got it together, while I figured it out.
They say if you love something, let it go;
If it comes back, it's yours.
That's how you know it's for keeps, yeah, it's for sure,
And you're ready and willin' to give me more than...
(To Chorus:)

Music

Recorded by Madonna

Words and Music by
MADONNA CICCONE and
MIRWAIS AHMADZAÏ
Arranged by Richard Bradley

Moderately fast ♩ = 120

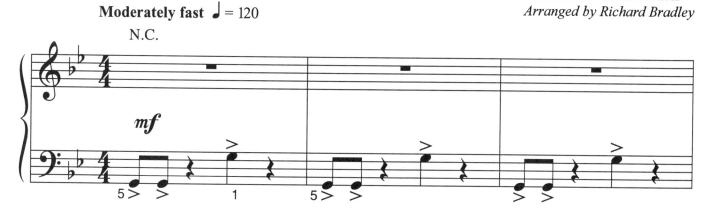

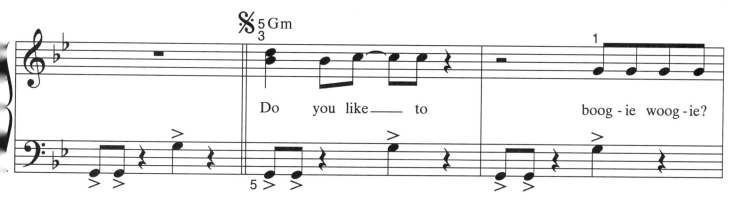

Do you like ____ to boog - ie woog - ie?

Do you like ____ to boog - ie woog - ie? Do you like ____ to

boog - ie woog - ie? Do you like ____ my ac - id rock?

Music - 5 - 1

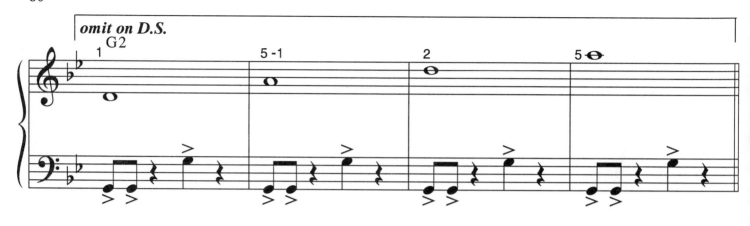

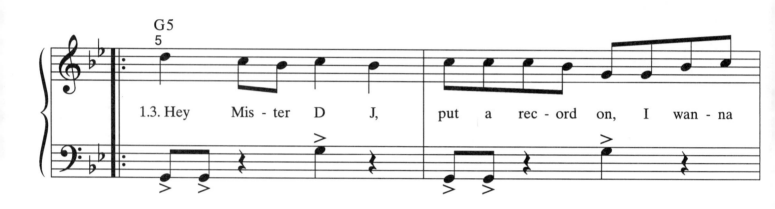

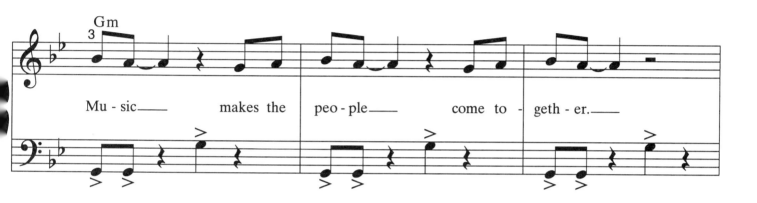

Mu - sic____ makes the peo - ple____ come to - geth - er.____

(Nev - er gon - na stop.) Mu - sic____ makes the bour - geoi - sie and the

reb - el.____ (Nev - er gon - na stop.) 2. Don't (Nev - er gon - na stop.)

Music - 5 - 3

Hey, Mis-ter D J.

D.S. 𝄋 *al Coda* ⊕

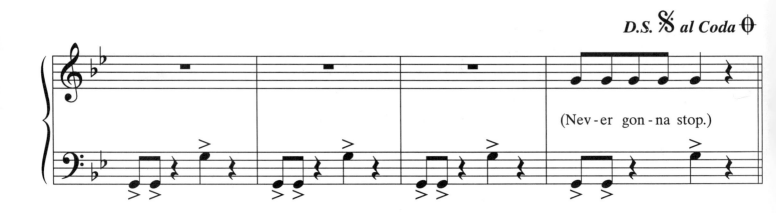

(Nev-er gon-na stop.)

Coda
⊕

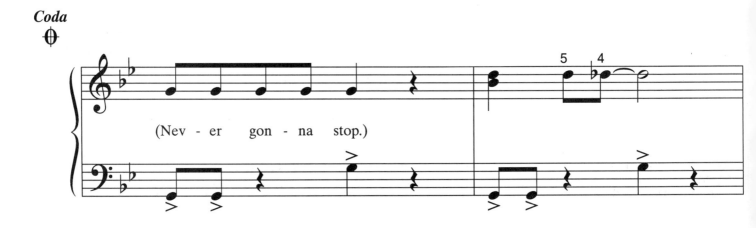

(Nev - er gon - na stop.)

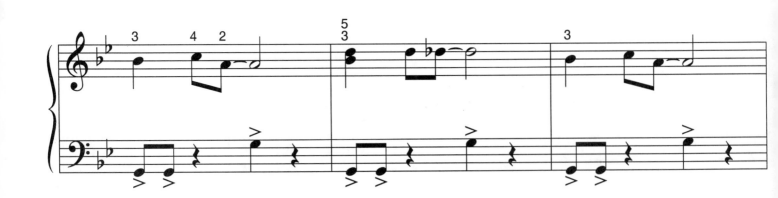

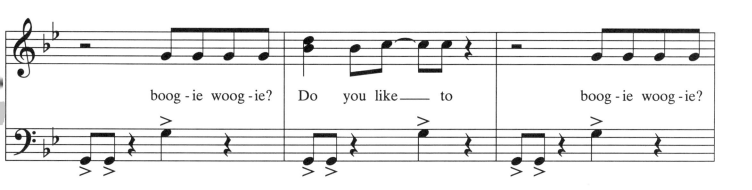

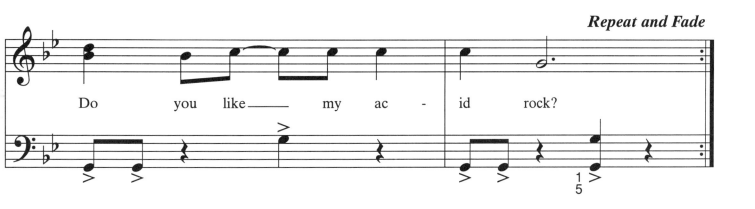

Verse 2:
Don't think of yesterday and I don't look at the clock.
I like to boogie woogie.
It's like riding on the wind and it never goes away,
Touches everything I'm in, got to have it every day.
(To Chorus:)

Music - 5 - 5

That's the Way It Is

Recorded by Celine Dion

Words and Music by
MAX MARTIN, KRISTIAN LUNDIN
and ANDREAS CARLSSON
Arranged by Richard Bradley

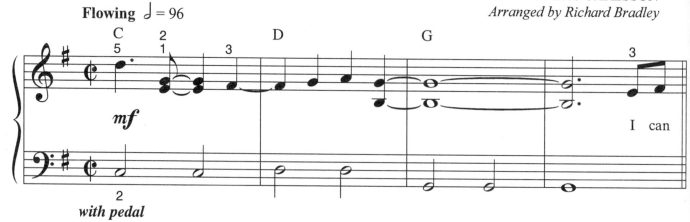

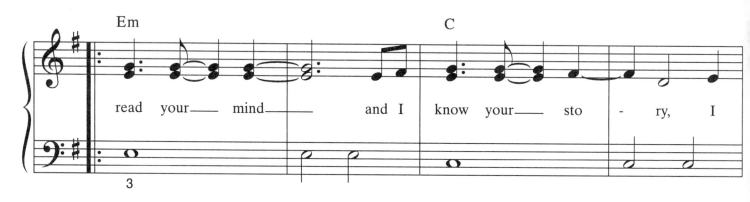

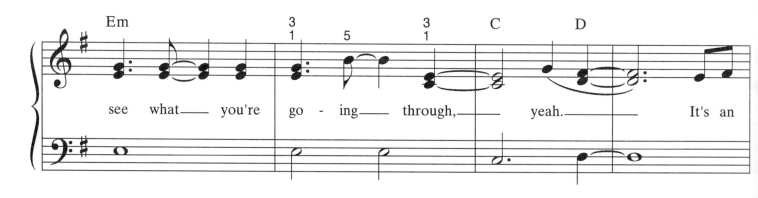

That's the Way It Is - 6 - 1

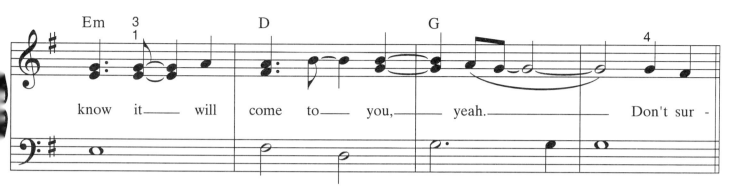

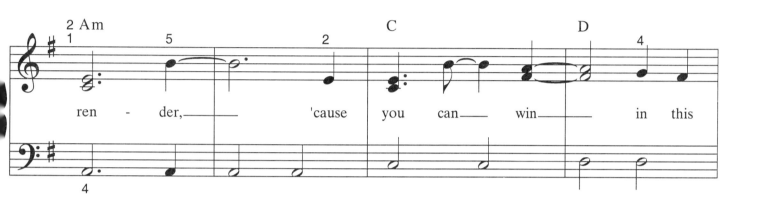

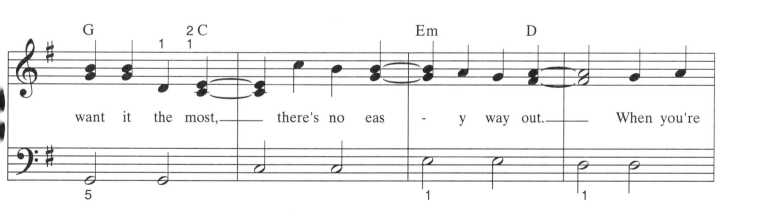

That's the Way It Is - 6 - 2

read - y to go____ and your heart's____ left in doubt,____ don't give

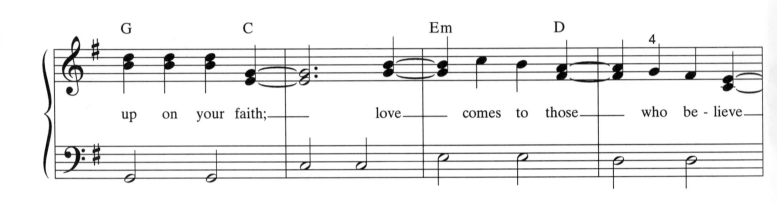

up on your faith;____ love____ comes to those____ who be - lieve____

___ it,____ and that's the____ way____ it is.____

When you____ That's the way____ it is.

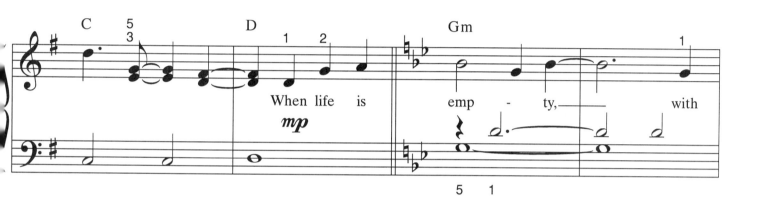

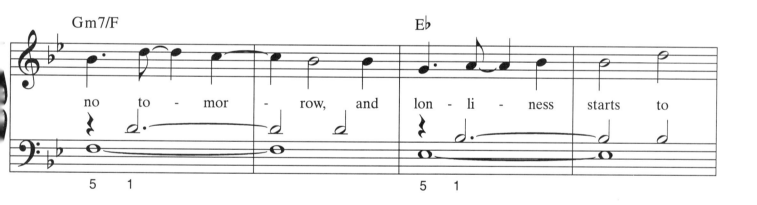

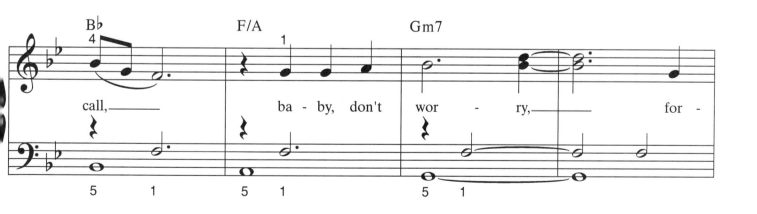

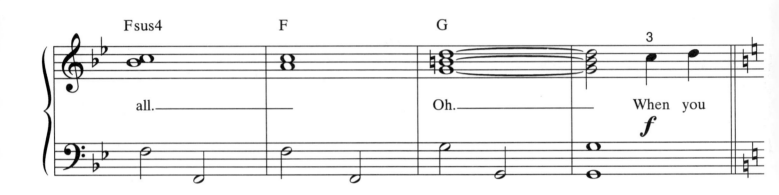

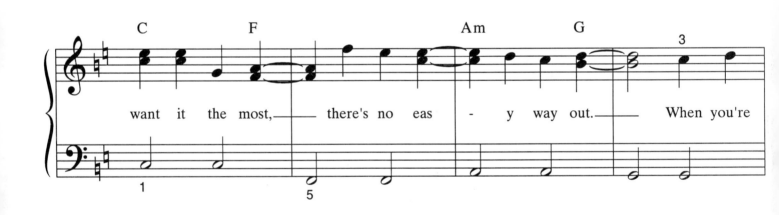

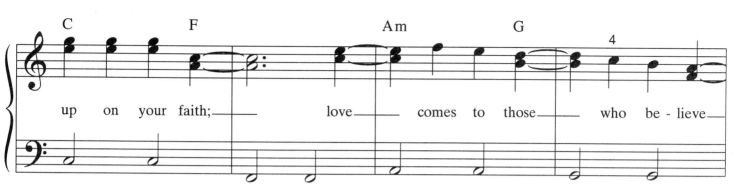

up on your faith;———— love—— comes to those—— who be - lieve——

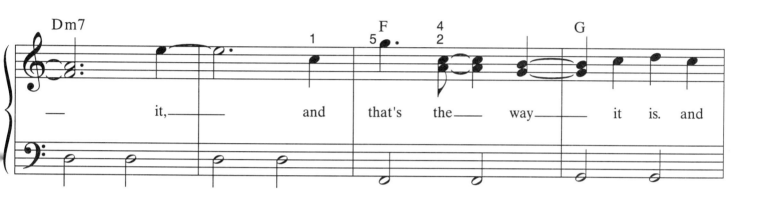

—— it,—— and that's the—— way—— it is. and

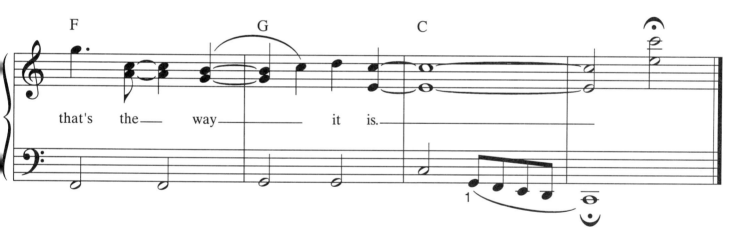

that's the—— way—— it is.————————

Verse 2:
When you question me for a simple answer,
I don't know what to say, no.
But it's plain to see, if you stick together,
You're gonna find the way, yeah.

As Long as You Love Me

Recorded by Backstreet Boys

By
MAX MARTIN
Arranged by Richard Bradley

As Long as You Love Me - 6 - 1

92

Chorus:

As Long as You Love Me - 6 - 4

Chorus:

Verse 3:
Every little thing that you have said and done
Feels like it's deep within me.
Doesn't really matter if you're on the run,
It seems like we're meant to be.

Oops! . . . I Did It Again

Recorded by Britney Spears

Words and Music by
MAX MARTIN and RAMI
Arranged by Richard Bradley

Oops!...I Did It Again - 4 - 1

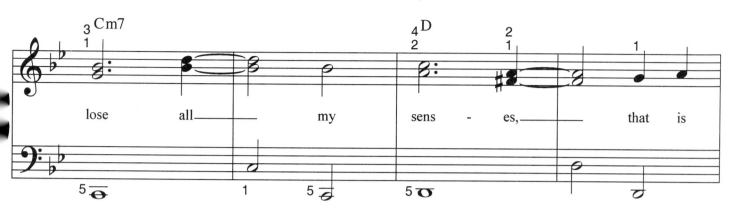

lose all_____ my sens - es,_____ that is

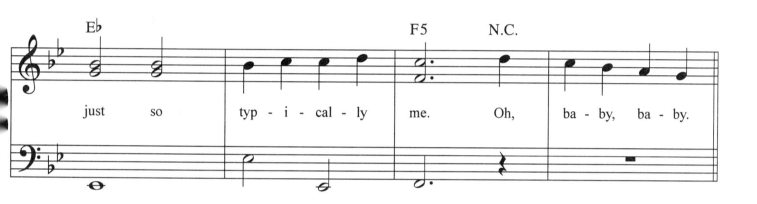

just so typ - i - cal - ly me. Oh, ba - by, ba - by.

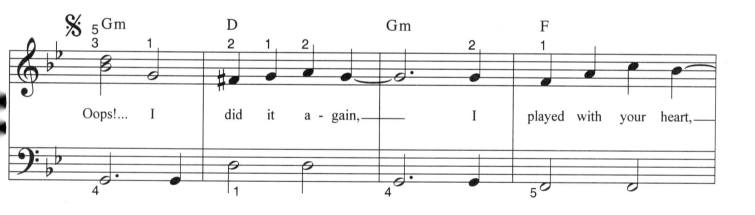

Oops!... I did it a - gain,_____ I played with your heart,_____

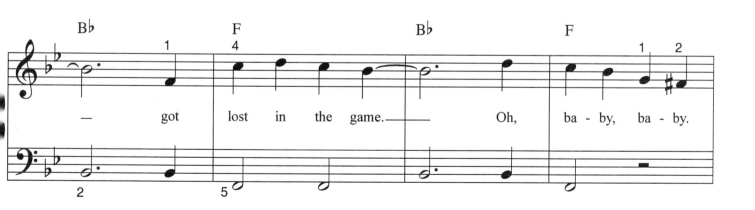

— got lost in the game._____ Oh, ba - by, ba - by.

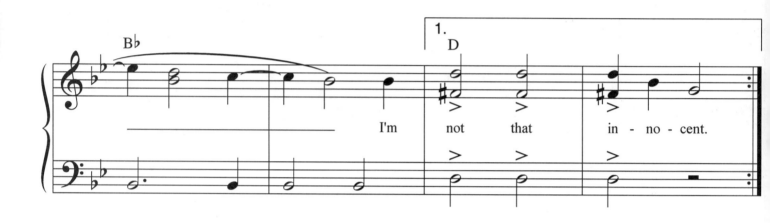

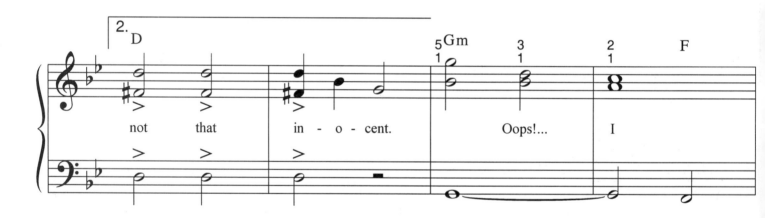

Verse 2:
You see my problem is this,
I'm dreaming away
Wishing that heroes, they truly exist.
I cry watching the days,
Can't you see I'm a fool, in so many ways?
But to . . .

It's Gonna Be Me

Recorded by ★NSYNC

Words and Music by
MAX MARTIN, RAMI
and ANDREAS CARLSSON
Arranged by Richard Bradley

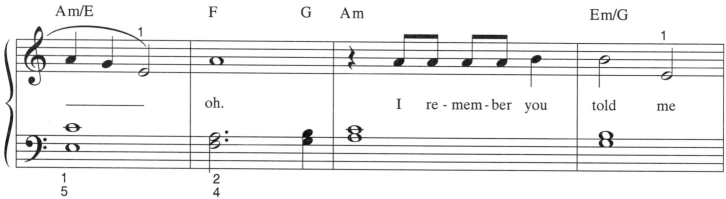

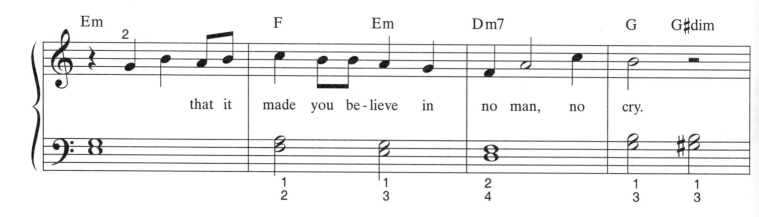

It's Gonna Be Me - 6 - 1

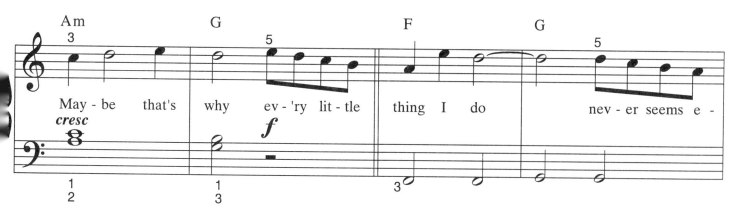

May - be that's why ev - 'ry lit - tle thing I do nev - er seems e -

cresc *f*

nough for you. You don't wan - na lose it a - gain, but

I'm not like them. Ba - by, when you fi - nal - ly——— get to

1.

love some - bod - y, guess—— what?—— It's gon - na be me.

102

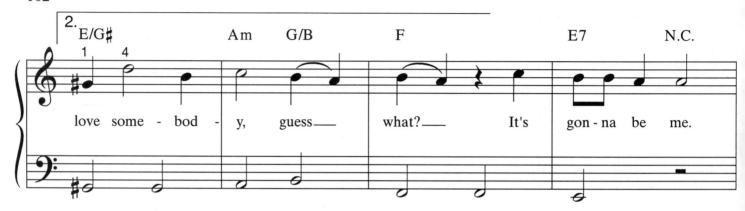

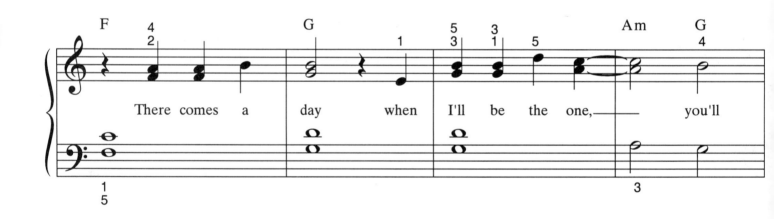

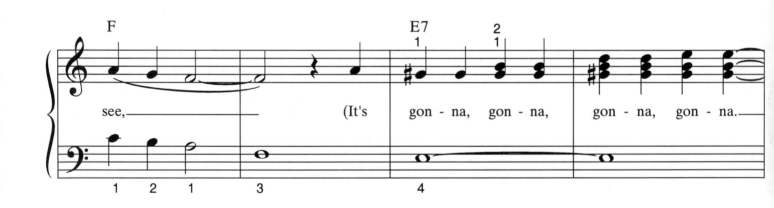

It's Gonna Be Me - 6 - 3

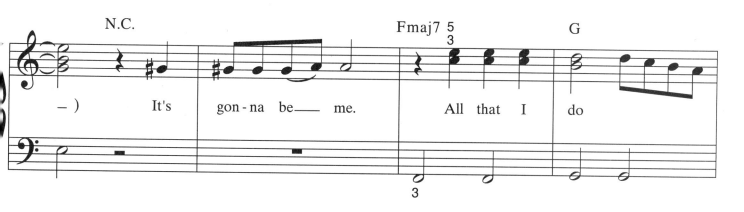

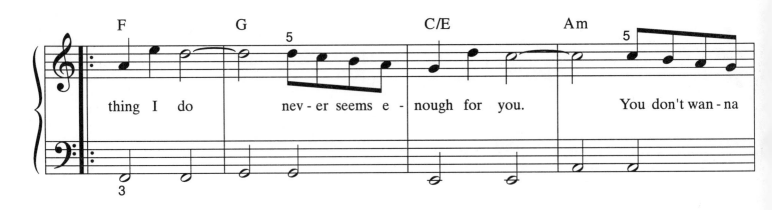

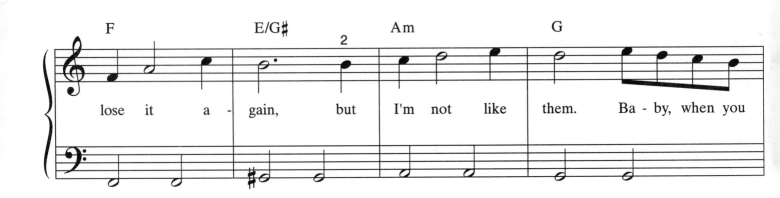

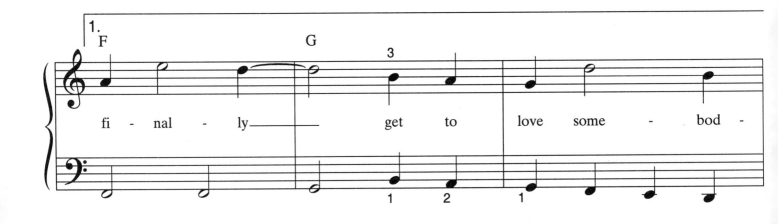

Verse 2:
You've got no choice, babe,
But to move on, you know
There ain't no time to waste,
'Cause you're just too blind to see.
But in the end you know it's gonna be me.
You can't deny,
So just tell me why...
(To Chorus:)

You Were Meant for Me

Recorded by Jewel

Words and Music by
JEWEL KILCHER and STEVE POLTZ
Arranged by Richard Bradley

I hear the clock, it's six A. M.,___ I feel so far___ from where I've been.___ I've got my eggs and my pan-cakes, too,___ I've got ma-ple syr-up, ev-'ry-thing but you.___

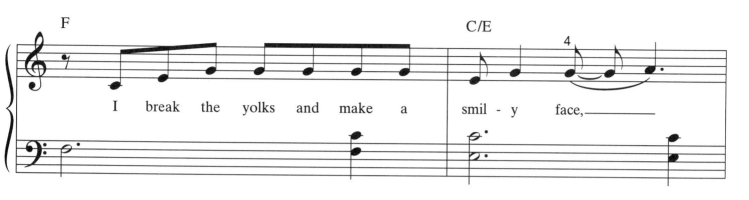

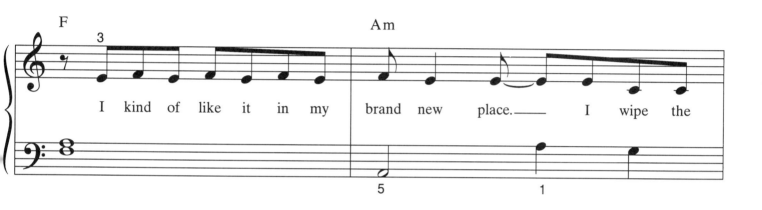

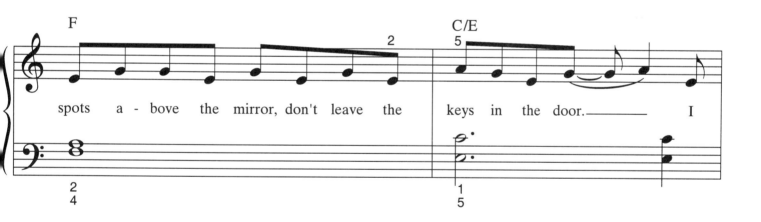

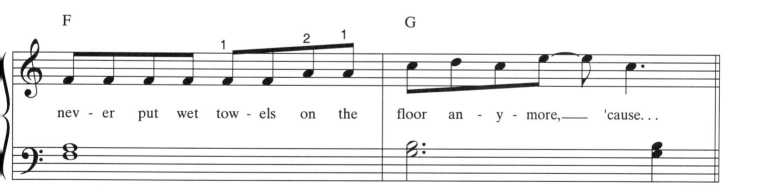

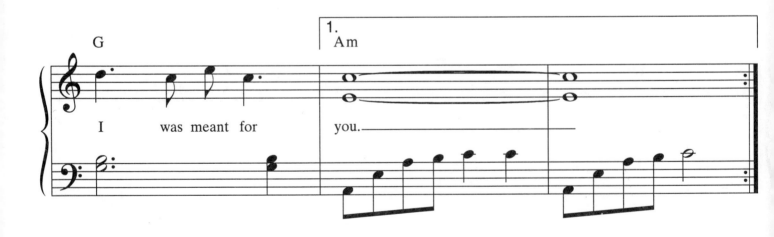

You Were Meant for Me - 5 - 3

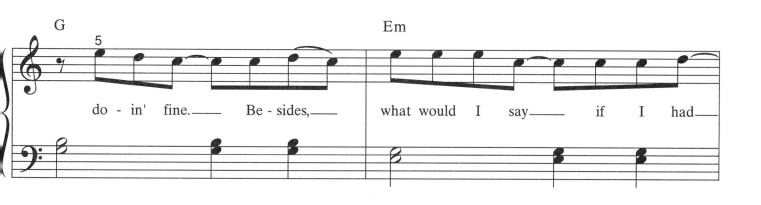

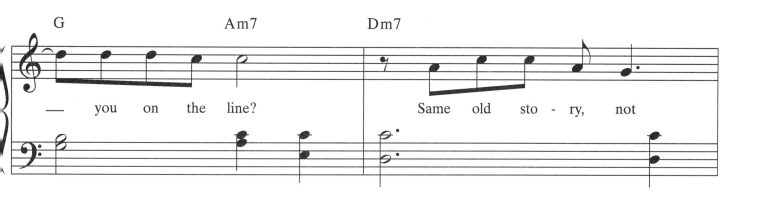

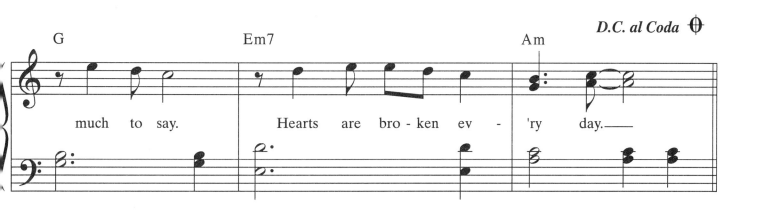

Coda

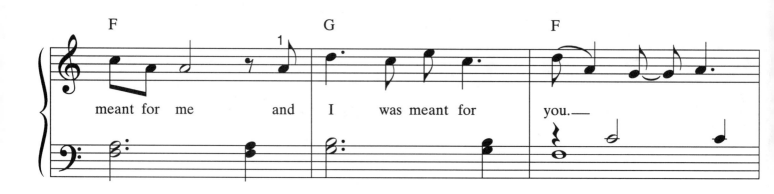

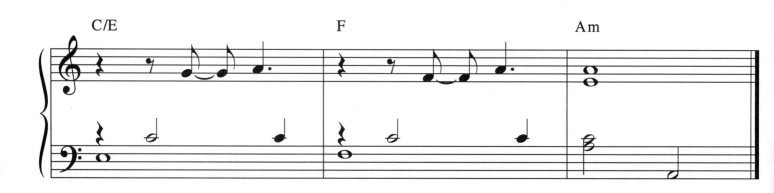

Verse 2:
I called my mama, she was out for a walk.
Consoled a cup of coffee, but it didn't wanna talk.
So I picked up a paper, it was more bad news,
More hearts being broken or people being used.
Put on my coat in the pouring rain.
I saw a movie, it just wasn't the same,
'Cause it was happy and I was sad,
And it made me miss you, oh, so bad.
(To Chorus:)

Verse 3:
I brush my teeth and put the cap back on,
I know you hate it when I leave the light on.
I pick a book up and then turn the sheets down,
And then I take a breath and a good look around.
Put on my pj's and hop into bed.
I'm half alive but I feel mostly dead.
I try and tell myself it'll be all right,
I just shouldn't think anymore tonight.
(To Chorus:)

She Bangs

Recorded by Ricky Martin

Words and Music by
ROBI ROSA, WALTER AFANASIEFF
and DESMOND CHILD
Arranged by Richard Bradley

1. Talk to me,—— tell me your name.——
2. Talk to me,—— tell me your sign.——

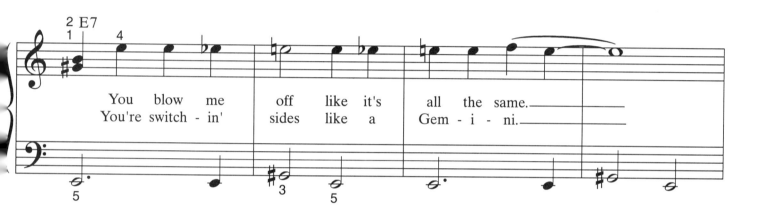

You blow me off like it's all the same.——
You're switch - in' sides like a Gem - i - ni.——

You lit a fuse, and now I'm tick - in' a - way—— like a bomb,
You're play - ing games and now you're hit - tin' my heart—— like a drum,

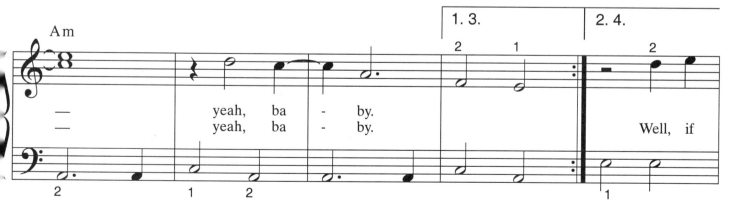

1. 3.
2. 4.

—— yeah, ba - by.
—— yeah, ba - by. Well, if

She Bangs - 5 - 1

112

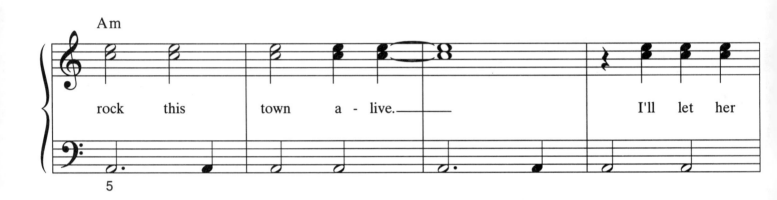

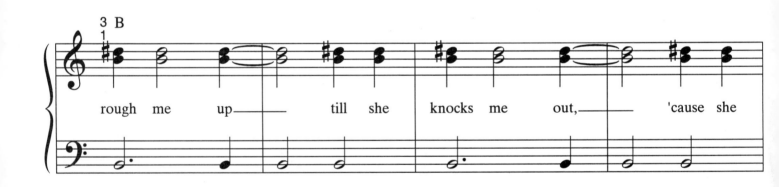

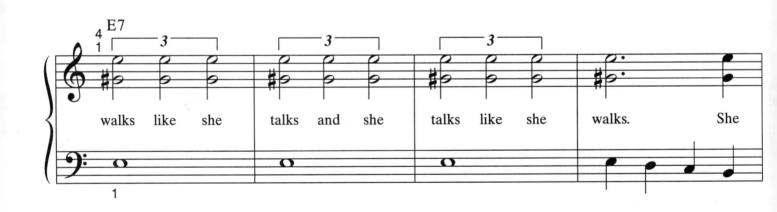

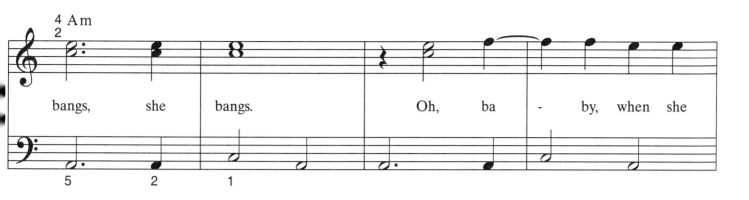

bangs,   she   bangs.   Oh,   ba   -   by,   when   she

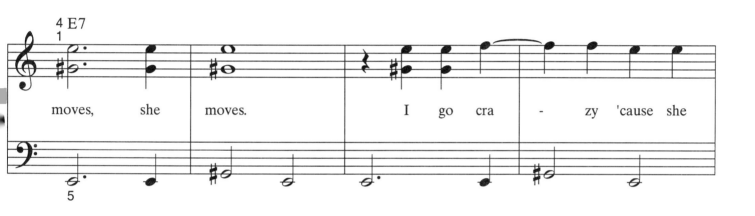

moves,   she   moves.   I   go   cra   -   zy   'cause   she

looks   like   a   flow - er,   but   she   stings   like   a   bee,

like   ev - 'ry   girl   in   his - to - ry._____   She

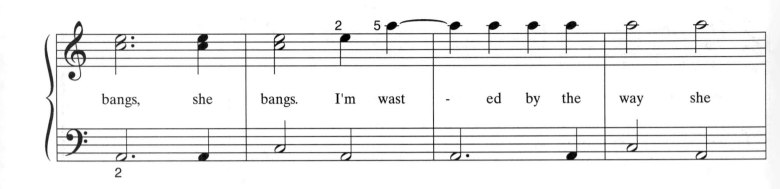

bangs,   she   bangs.   I'm   wast - ed   by the   way   she

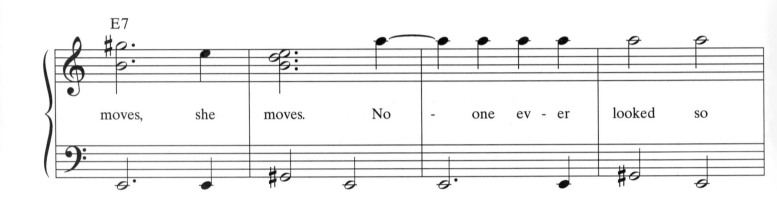

moves,   she   moves.   No - one ev - er   looked   so

fine.   She re - minds___   me that a

wom - an's   got   one   thing   on   her   mind.___

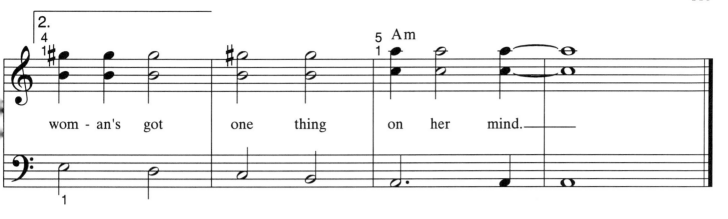

wom - an's got one thing on her mind.

Verse 3:
Talk to me, tell me your name.
I'm just a link in your daisy chain.
Your rap sounds like a diamond map
To the stars, yeah, baby.

Verse 4:
Talk to me, tell me the news.
You'll wear me out like a pair of shoes.
We'll dance until the band goes home,
Then you're gone, yeah, baby.
Well, if it looks like love should be a crime,
You'd better lock me up for life.
I'll do the time with a smile on my face,
Thinkin' of her in her leather and lace.

I Do (Cherish You)

Recorded by 98°

Words and Music by
KEITH STEGALL and DAN HILL
Arranged by Richard Bradley

Moderately slow ♩ = 80

I do, I do, babe. I do, I do.——

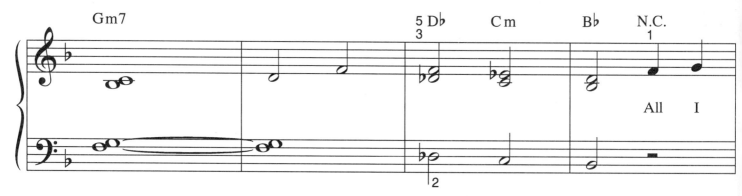

All I

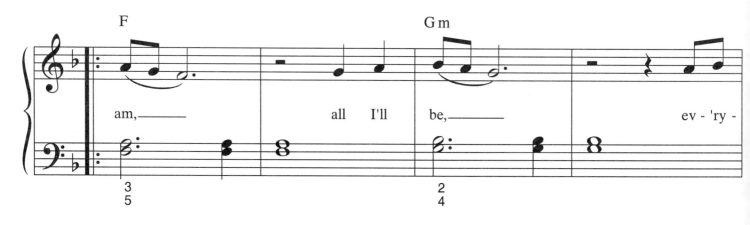

am,—— all I'll be,—— ev - 'ry -

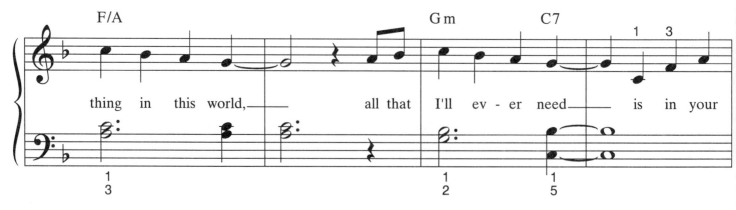

thing in this world,—— all that I'll ev - er need—— is in your

I Do (Cherish You) - 6 - 1

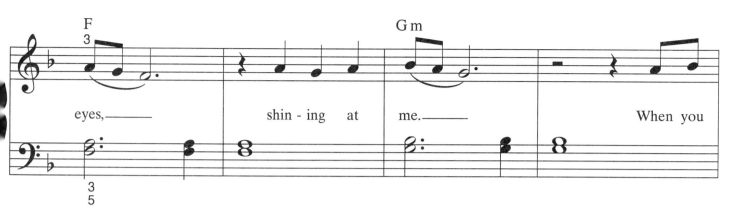

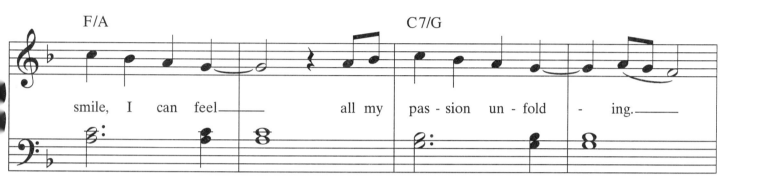

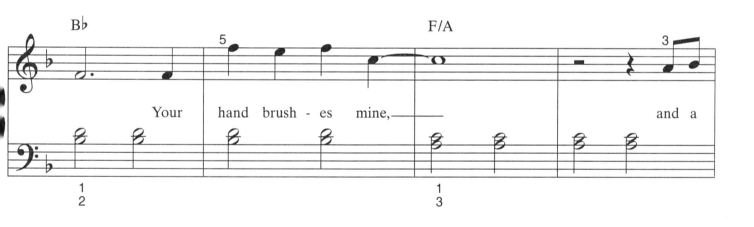

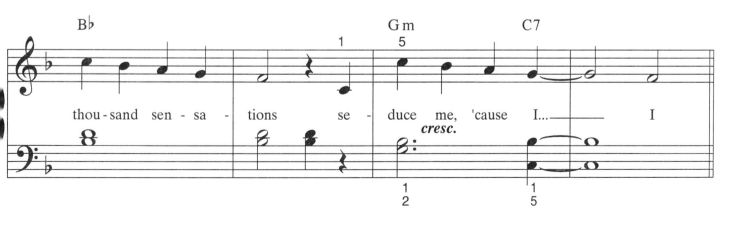

118

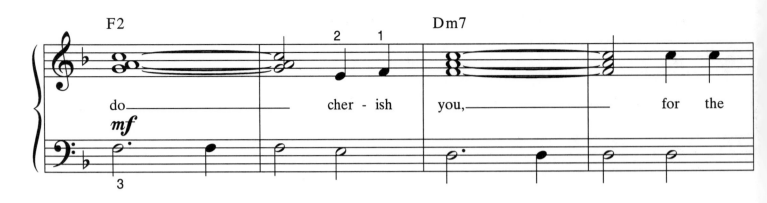

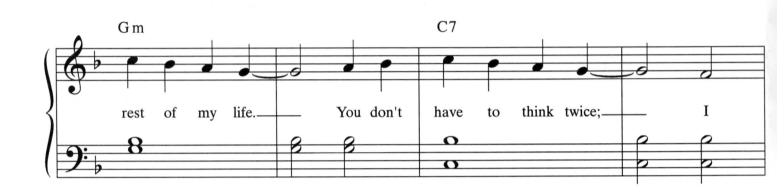

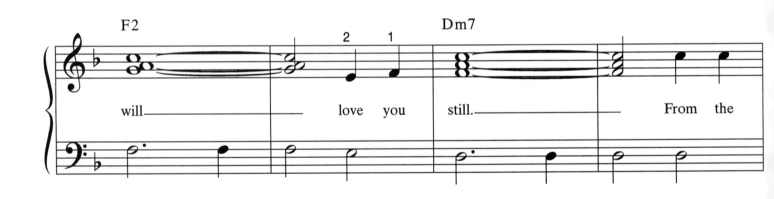

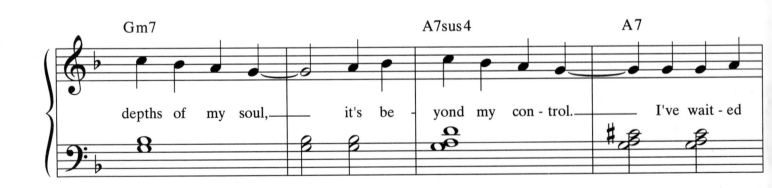

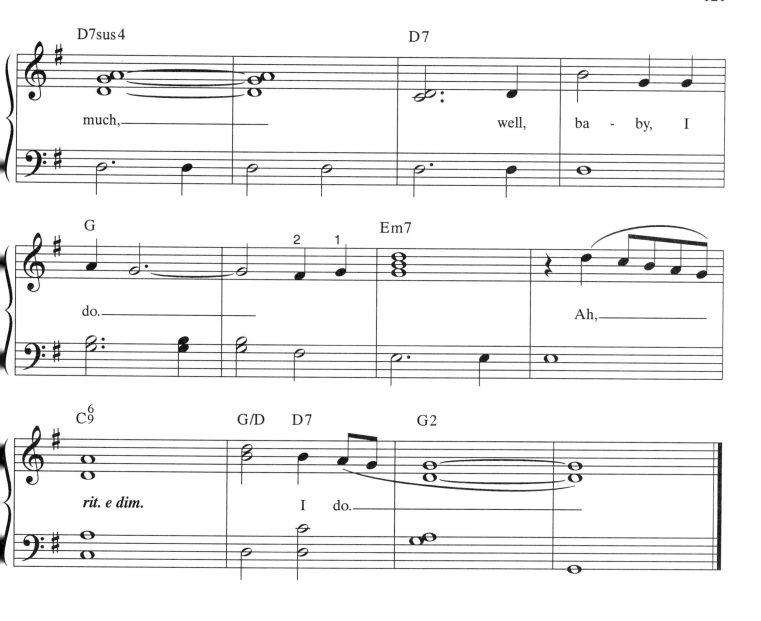

Verse 2:
In my world before you,
I lived outside my emotions.
Didn't know where I was going
Till that day I found you.
How you opened my life
To a new paradise.
In a world torn by change,
Still with all of my heart,
Till my dying day . . .
(To Chorus:)

Shape of My Heart

Recorded by Backstreet Boys

Words and Music by
MAX MARTIN. RAMI
and LISA MISKOVSKY
Arranged by Richard Bradley

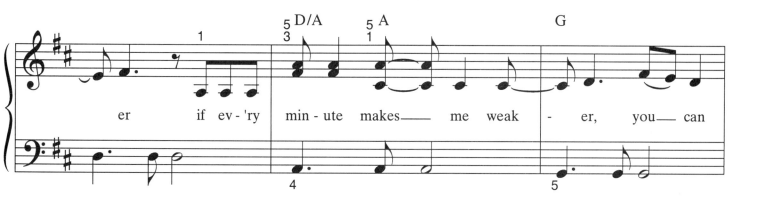

er   if ev - 'ry   min - ute makes____ me weak   - er,   you__ can

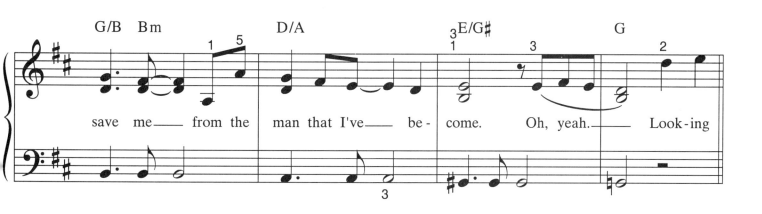

save me____ from the   man that I've____ be - come.   Oh, yeah.____ Look-ing

Chorus:

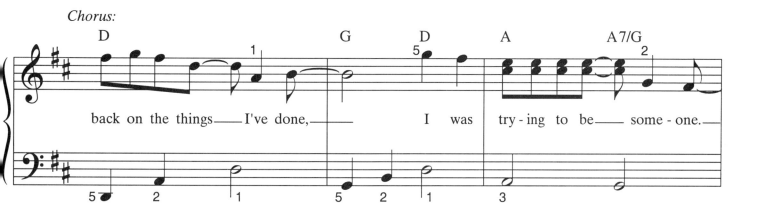

back on the things____I've done,____   I   was   try - ing to be____ some - one.____

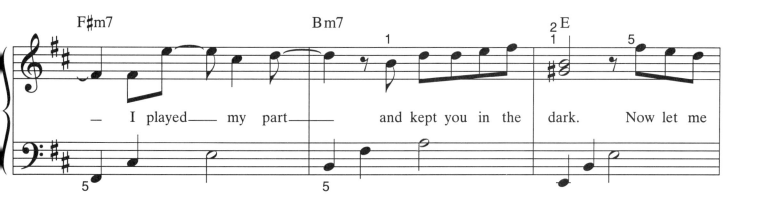

— I played____ my part____   and kept you in the   dark.   Now let me

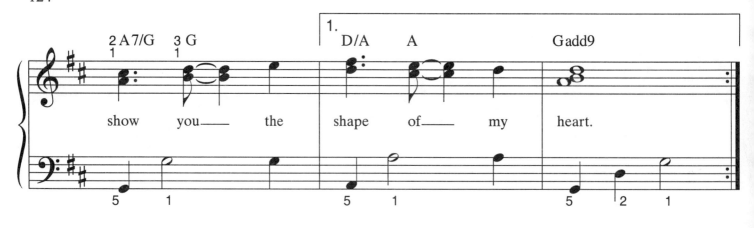

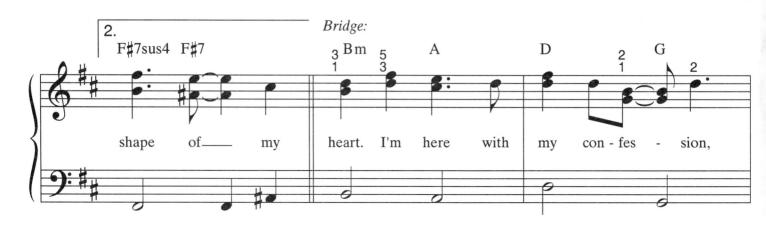

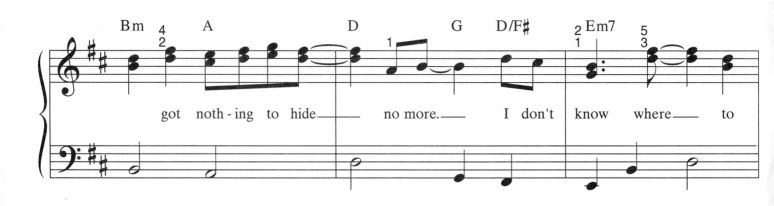

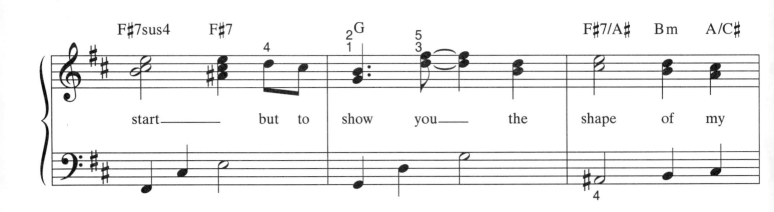

Verse 2:
Sadness is beautiful.
Loneliness is tragical.
So help me, I can't win this war.
Touch me now,
Don't bother if every second makes me weaker,
You can save me from the man that I've become.
Oh, yeah. Looking. . .
(To Chorus)

I Turn to You

Recorded by Christina Aguilera

Words and Music by
DIANE WARREN
Arranged by Richard Bradley

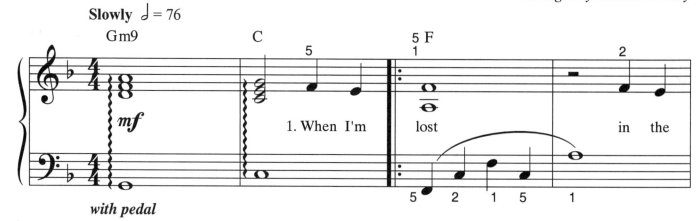

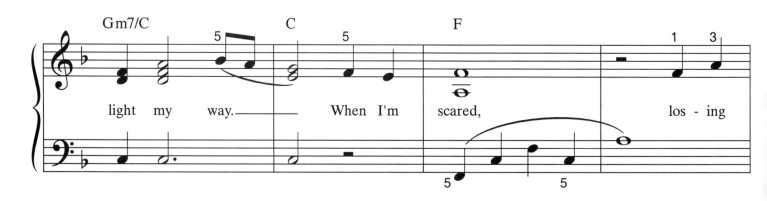

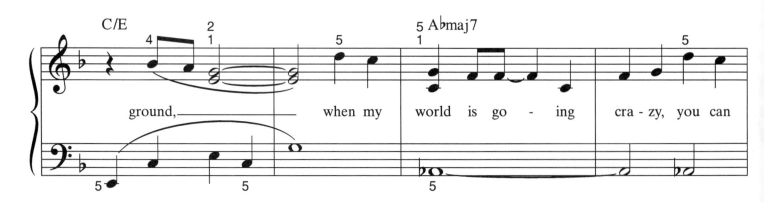

I Turn to You - 6 - 1

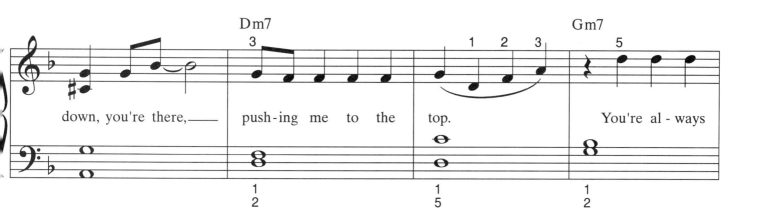

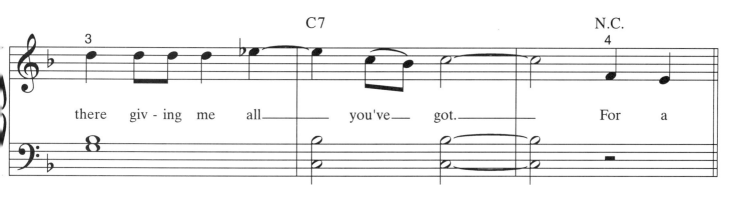

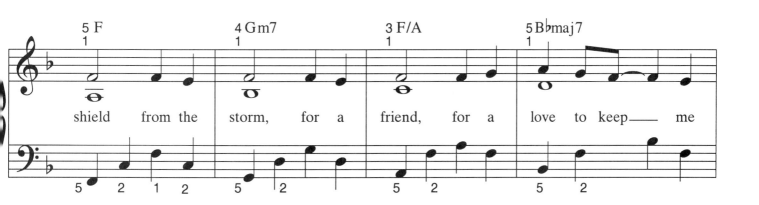

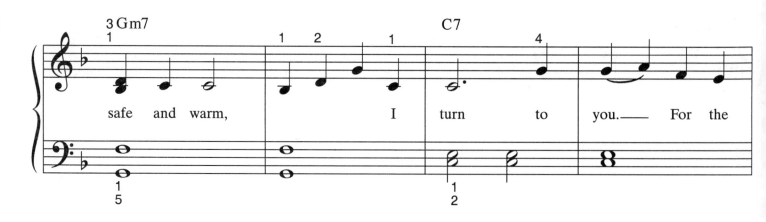

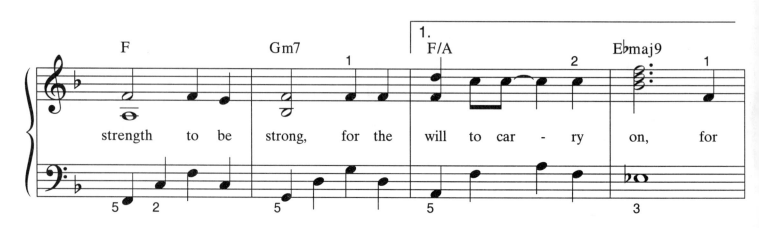

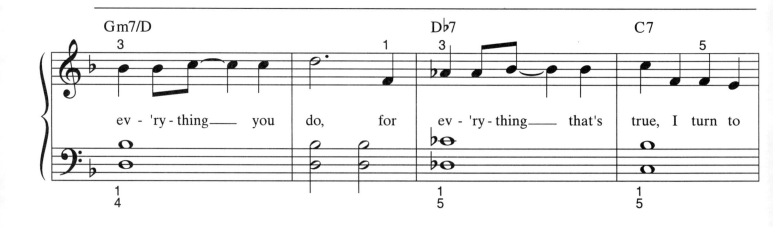

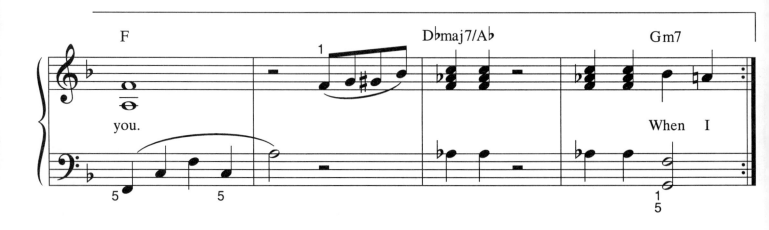

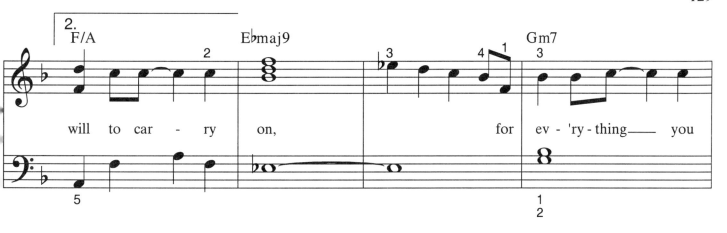

will to car - ry on, for ev - 'ry-thing___ you

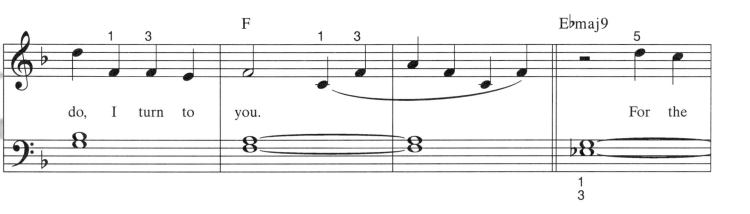

do, I turn to you. For the

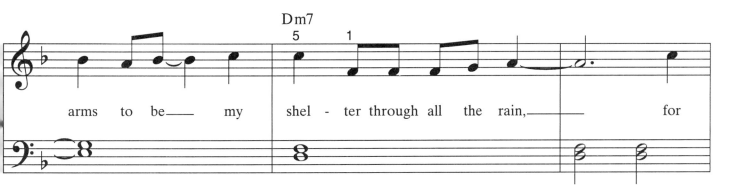

arms to be___ my shel - ter through all the rain,___ for

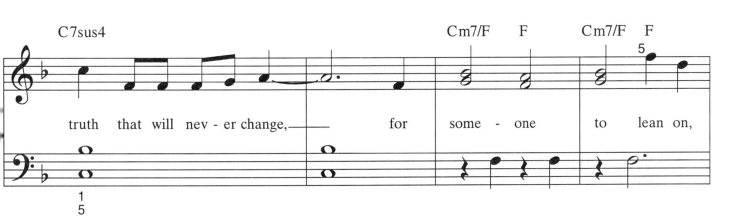

truth that will nev - er change,___ for some - one to lean on,

I Turn to You - 6 - 4

Verse 2:
When I lose the will to win,
I just reach for you
And I can reach the sky again.
I can do anything
'Cause your love is so amazing,
'Cause your love inspires me.
And when I need a friend,
You're always on my side,
Giving me faith,
Taking me through the night.

Believe

Recorded by Cher

Words and Music by
BRIAN HIGGINS, STUART McLENNAN, PAUL BARRY
STEPHEN TORCH, MATT GRAY and TIM POWELL
Arranged by Richard Bradley

Moderate disco beat ♩ = 132

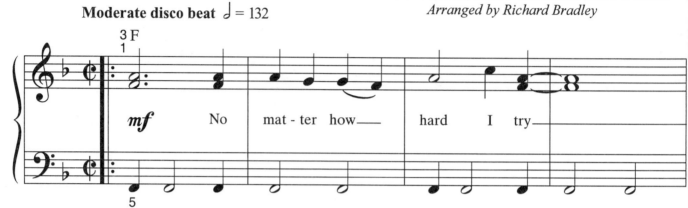

mf No mat-ter how— hard I try—

— you keep push-ing me a-side— and I can't

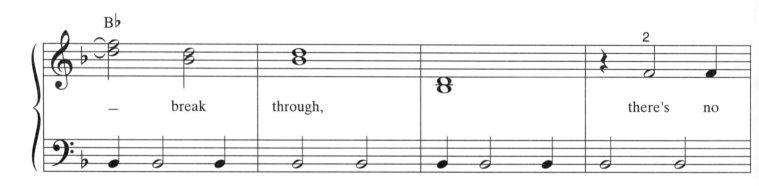

— break through, there's no

talk-ing to you.— It's so

Believe - 6 - 1

sad_____ that you're leav - ing,_____ takes

time_____ to be - lieve___ it,____

but af - ter all is said and done,____

you're goin' to be the lone - ly one,___ oh.___

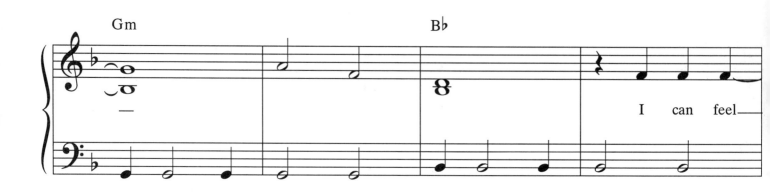

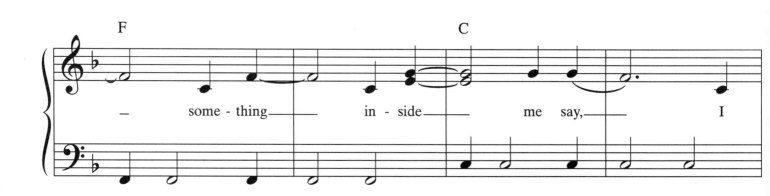

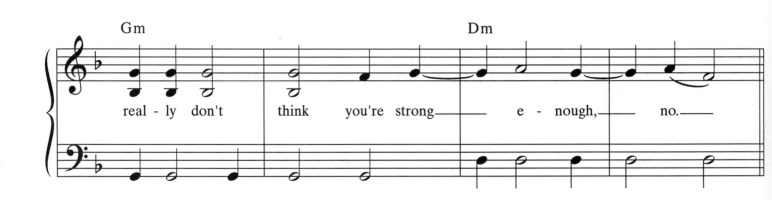

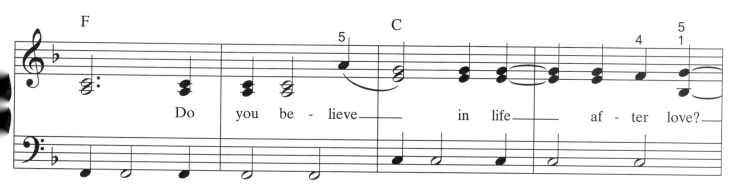

Do you be - lieve ___ in life ___ af - ter love?

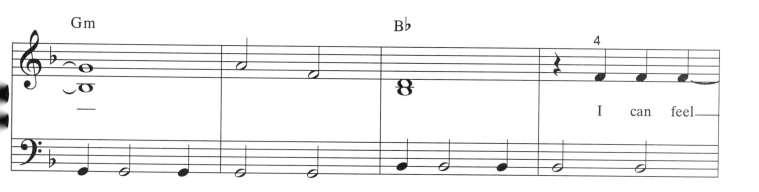

— I can feel ___

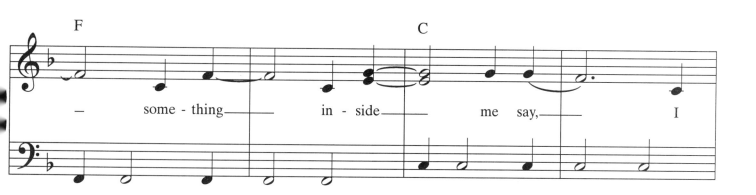

— some - thing ___ in - side ___ me say, ___ I

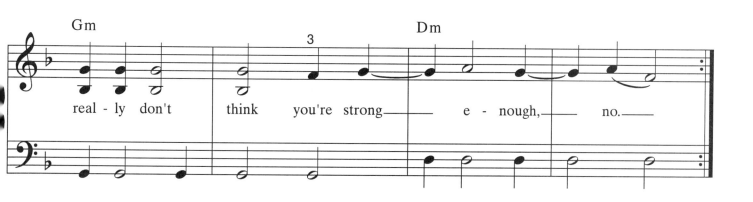

real - ly don't think you're strong ___ e - nough, ___ no. ___

Believe - 6 - 4

136

Believe - 6 - 5

Verse 2:
What am I supposed to do,
Sit around and wait for you,
And I can't do that,
There's no turning back.
I need time to move on
I need love to feel strong,
'Cause I've had time to think it through,
And maybe I'm too good for you, oh.

Genie in a Bottle

Recorded by Christina Aguilera

Words and Music by
PAMELA SHEYNE. DAVID FRANK
and STEVE KIPNER
Arranged by Richard Bradley

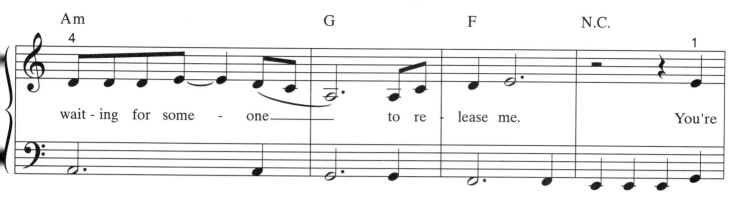

waiting for some - one to re - lease me. You're

lick-in' your lips and blow-ing kiss-es my way, but that don't mean I'm gon - na

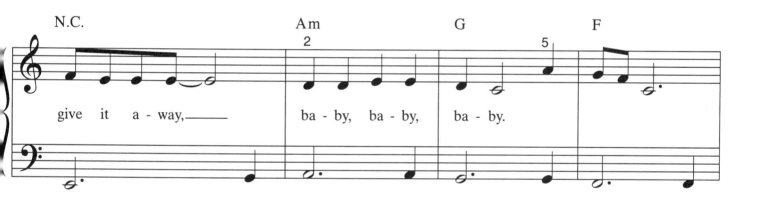

give it a - way, ba - by, ba - by, ba - by.

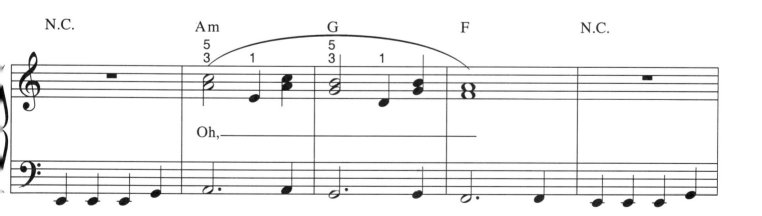

Oh,

140

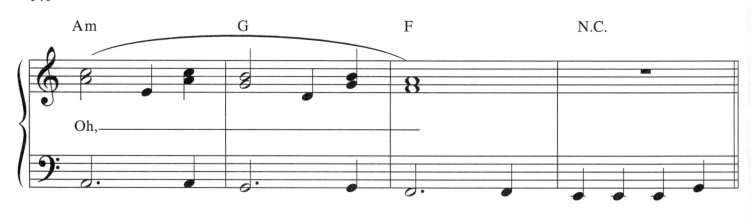

Oh,

If you want to be with me, ba - by, there's a price to

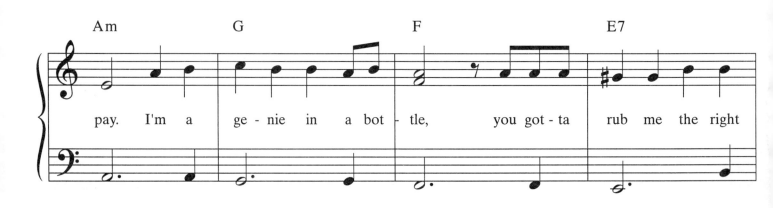

pay. I'm a ge - nie in a bot - tle, you got - ta rub me the right

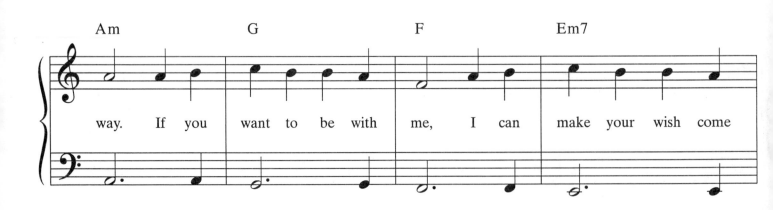

way. If you want to be with me, I can make your wish come

Genie in a Bottle - 5 - 3

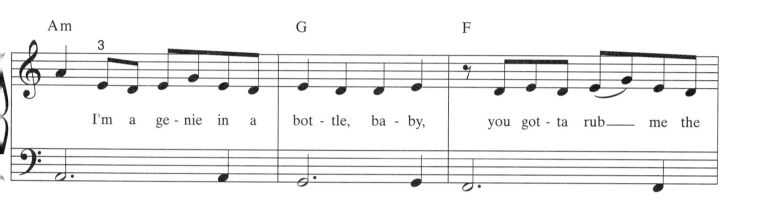

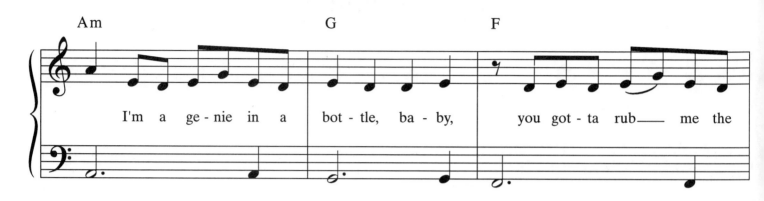

Verse 2:
The music's playing and the light's down low.
Just one more dance and then we're good to go.
Waiting for someone who needs me.
Hormones racing at the speed of light,
But that don't mean it's got to be tonight,
Baby, baby, baby.

Chorus 2:
If you want to be with me, baby, there's a price to pay.
I'm a genie in a bottle, you got to rub me the right way.
If you want to be with me, I can make your wish come true.
Just come and set me free, and, baby, I'll be with you.

My Everything

Recorded by 98°

Words and Music by
ARNTHOR BIRGISSON, ANDERS SVEN BAGGE,
NICK LACHEY and ANDREW LACHEY
Arranged by Richard Bradley

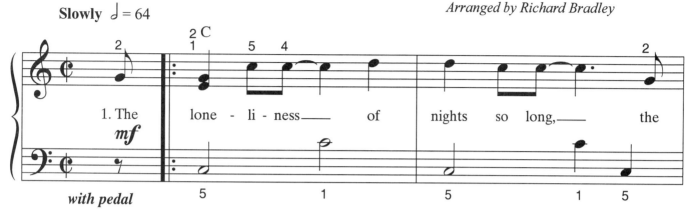

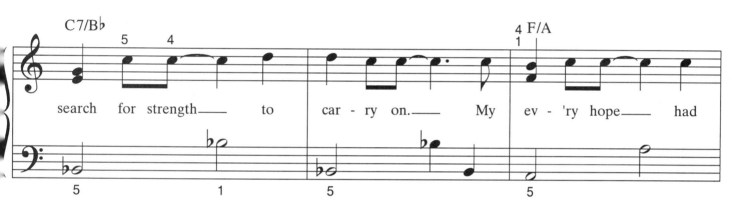

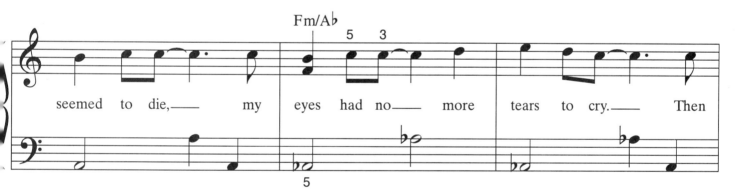

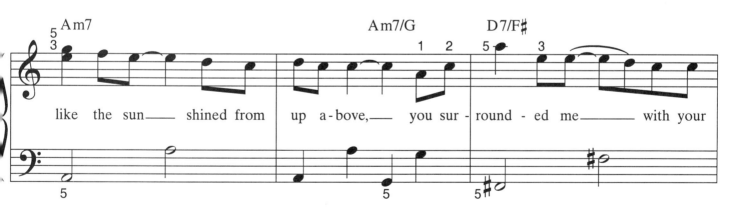

My Everything - 5 - 1

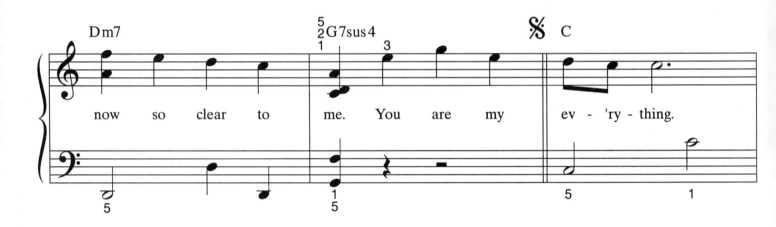

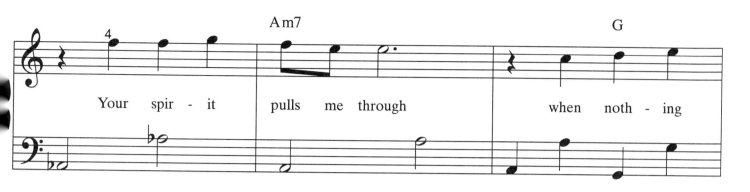

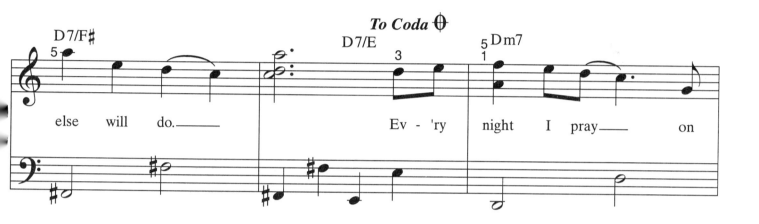

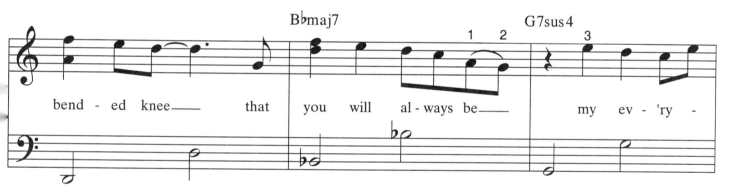

My Everything - 5 - 3

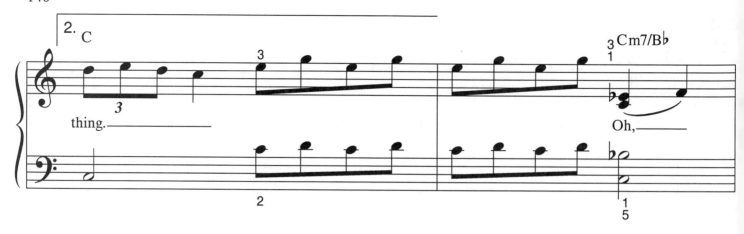

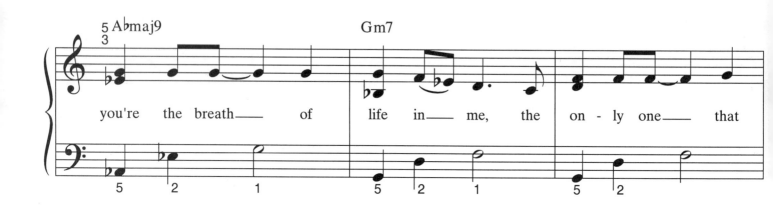

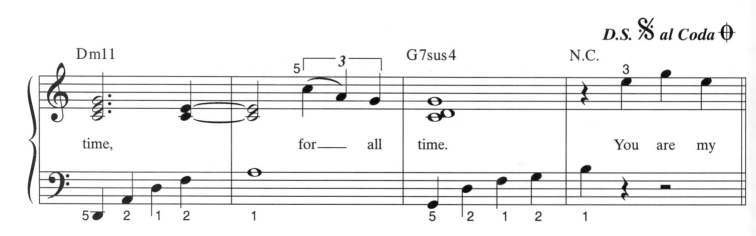

Coda

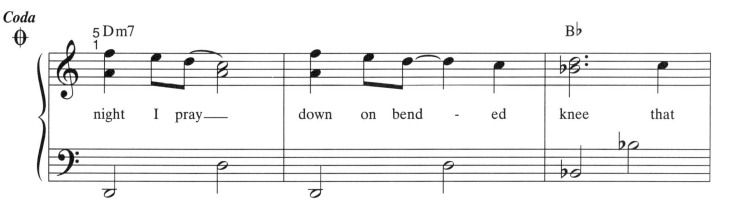

night I pray___ down on bend - ed knee that

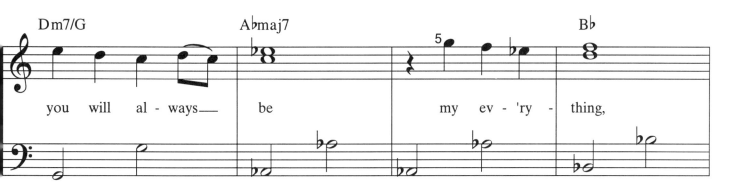

you will al - ways___ be my ev - 'ry - thing,

oh, my ev - e - ry - thing.___

Verse 2:
Now all my hopes and all my dreams are suddenly reality.
You've opened up my heart to feel a kind of love that's truly real.
A guiding light that'll never fade.
There's not a thing in life that I would ever trade.
For the love you give and won't let go,
I hope you'll always know...
(To Chorus:)

Smooth

Recorded by Santana featuring Rob Thomas

Music by ITAAL SHUR and ROB THOMAS
Lyrics by ROB THOMAS
Arranged by Richard Bradley

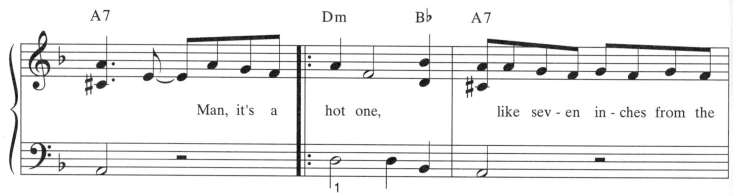

Smooth - 4 - 1

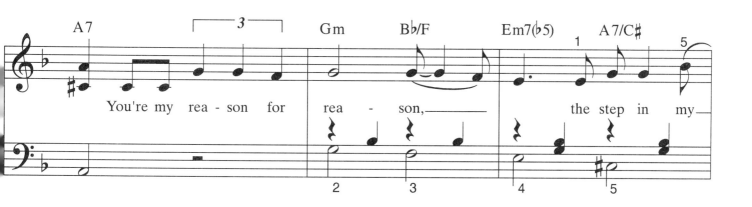

Smooth - 4 - 2

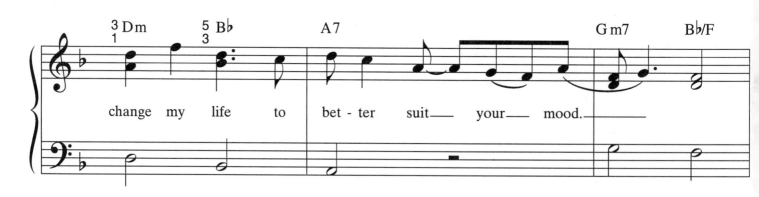

change my life to bet - ter suit___ your___ mood.___

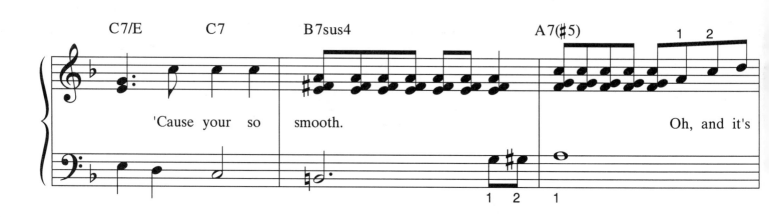

'Cause your so smooth. Oh, and it's

just like the o - cean un - der the moon.___ Well, it's the same as the e - mo - tion that I

get from you.___ You got the kind of lov-ing that can be so smooth,___ yeah.

Smooth - 4 - 3

Verse 2:
Well, I'll tell you one thing,
If you would leave, it be a crying shame.
In every breath and every word.
I hear your name calling me out, yeah.
Well, out from the barrio,
You hear my rhythm on your radio.
You feel the tugging of the world,
So soft and slow, turning you 'round and 'round.

I'm Already There

Recorded by Lonestar

Words and Music by
GARY BAKER, FRANK J. MYERS
and RICHIE McDONALD
Arranged by Richard Bradley

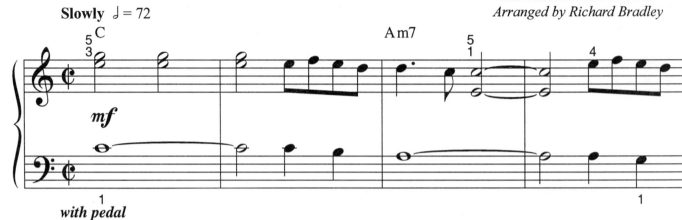

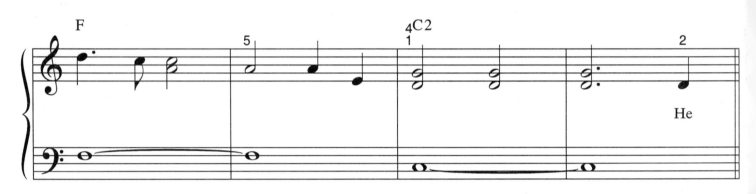

called her on___ the road from a lone - ly, cold___ ho -

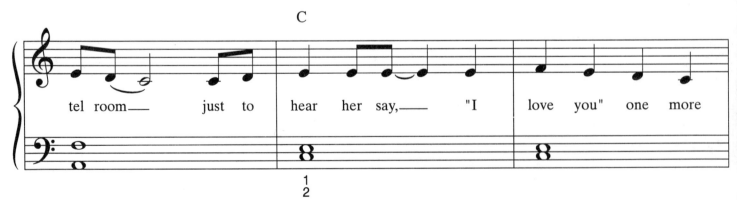

tel room___ just to hear her say,___ "I love you" one more

I'm Already There - 6 - 1

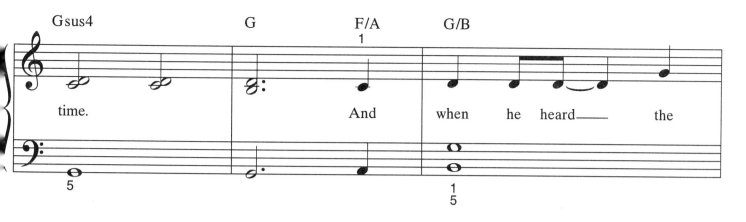

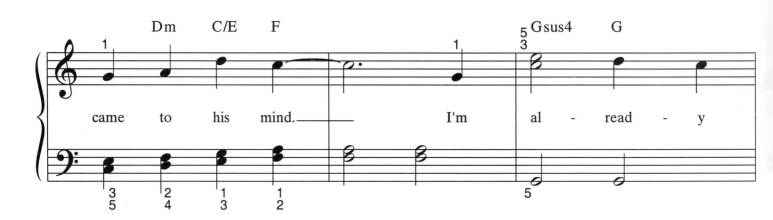

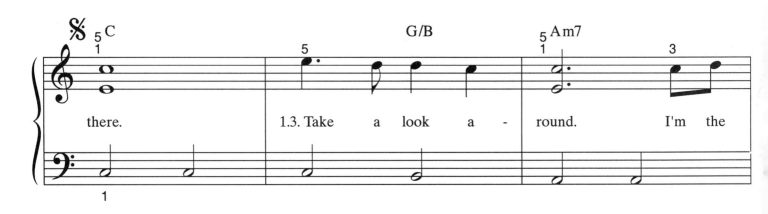

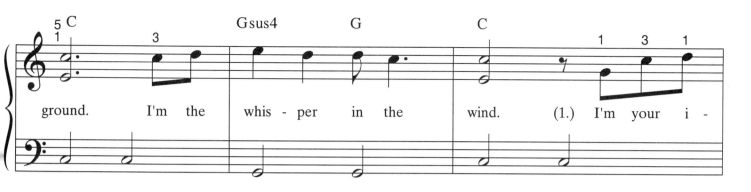

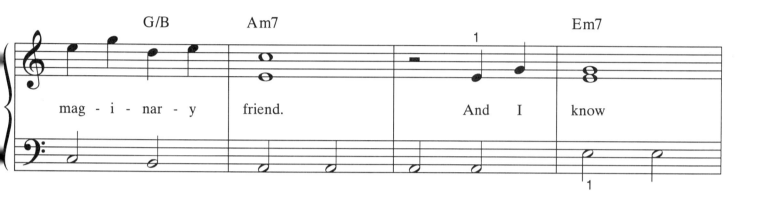

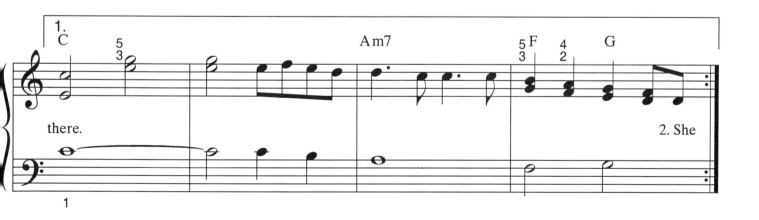

I'm Already There - 6 - 4

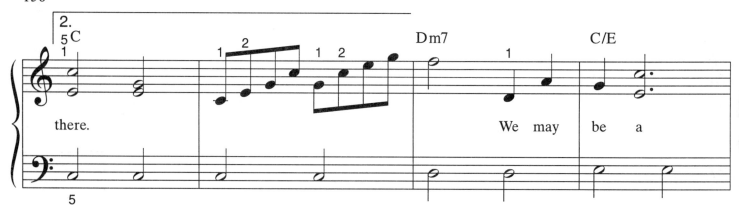

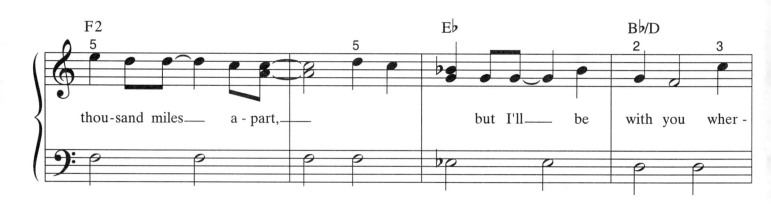

al - read - y   there.

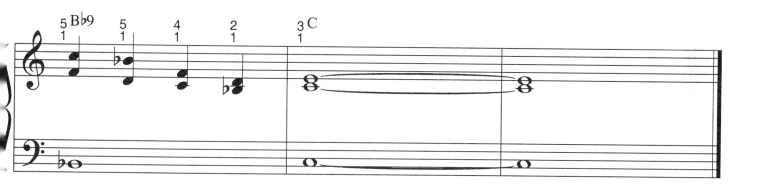

Verse 2:
She got back on the phone, said, "I really miss you, darlin.'
Don't worry about the kids, they'll be alright.
Wish I was in your arms, lyin' right there beside you.
But I know that I'll be in your dreams tonight.
And I'll gently kiss your lips, touch you with my fingertips.
So turn out the light and close your eyes."
I'm already there. Don't make a sound.
I'm the beat in your heart. I'm the moonlight shinning down.
I'm the whisper in the wind. (2.3.) And I'll be there 'til the end.
Can you feel the love that we share?
Oh, I'm already there.

She's All I Ever Had

Recorded by Ricky Martin

Words and Music by
ROBI ROSA, GEORGE NORIEGA
and JON SECADA
Arranged by Richard Bradley

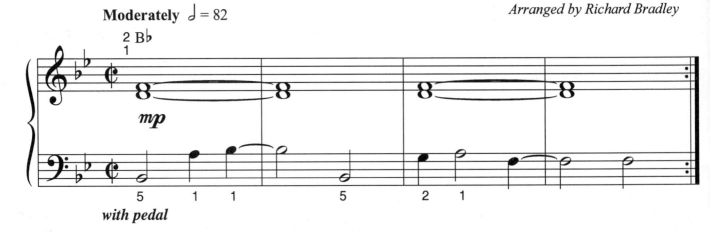

with pedal

Here I am,   bro - ken wings.

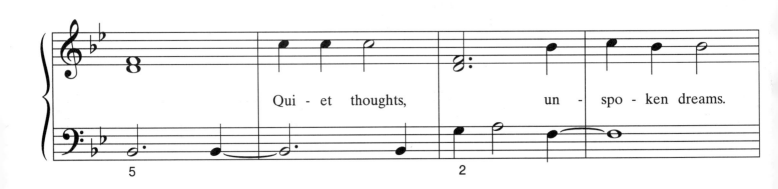

Qui - et thoughts,   un - spo - ken dreams.

Here I am,   a - lone a - gain.

She's All I Ever Had - 6 - 1

I need her now ___ to hold my hand.

She's all, ___ she is all I ev-er

had. ___ She's the air ___ I breathe. ___

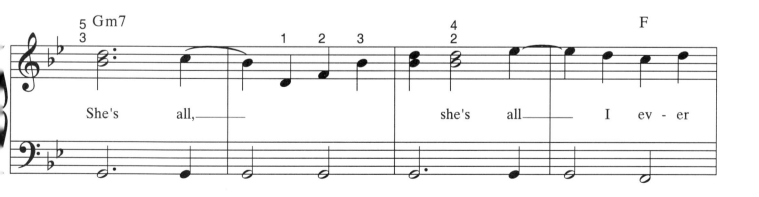

She's all, ___ she's all ___ I ev - er

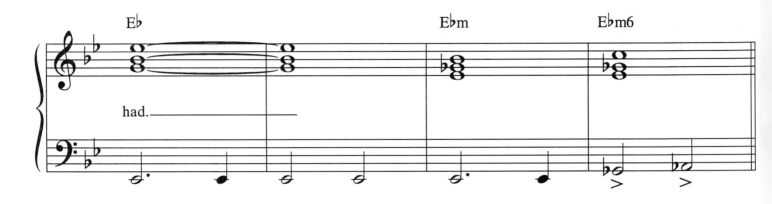

Chorus:

It's the way she makes me feel, it's the on - ly thing that's

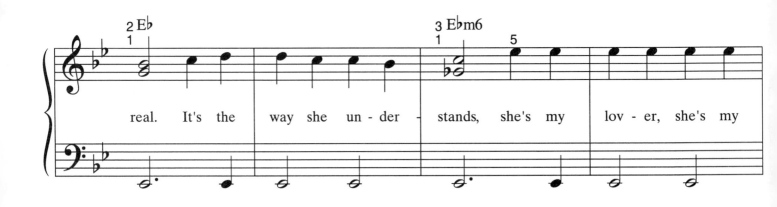

real. It's the way she un - der - stands, she's my lov - er, she's my

friend. When I look in - to her eyes, it's the way I feel in -

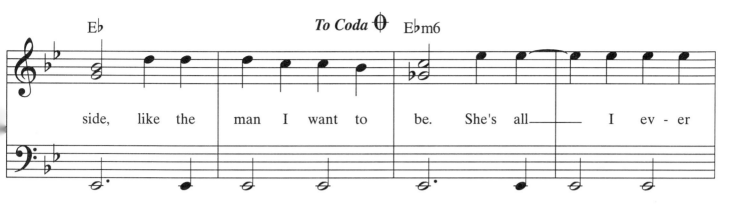

side, like the   man   I   want   to   be.   She's   all⎯⎯   I   ev - er

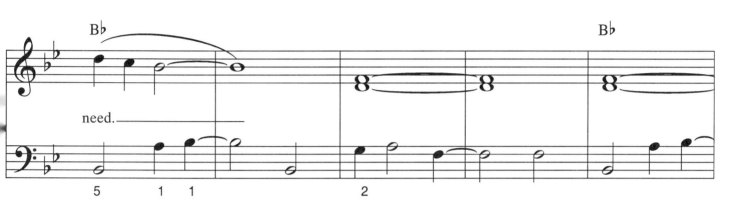

need.⎯⎯⎯⎯

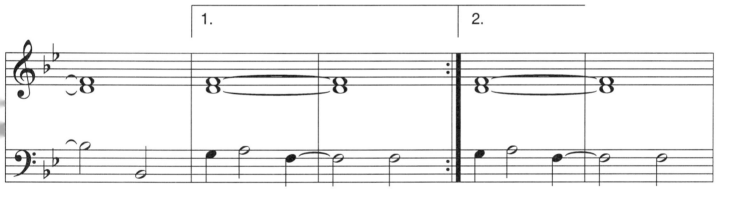

162

Verse 2:
So much time, so much pain,
There's one thing still remains.
The way she cared, the love we shared.
And through it all, she's always been there.
She's all, she is all I ever had.
In a world so cold, so empty,
She's all, she's all I ever had.
(To Chorus:)

Verse 3:
She's all, she is all I ever had.
I have to make her see, yeah.
She's all I ever had.

Back at One

Recorded by Brian McKnight

Words and Music by
BRIAN McKNIGHT
Arranged by Richard Bradley

Back at One - 4 - 1

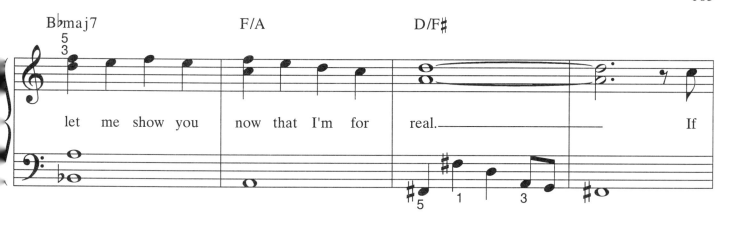

let me show you now that I'm for real._____ If

all things___ in time, time will re - veal.___ Yeah.___

One, you're like a dream come true. Two, just wan - na

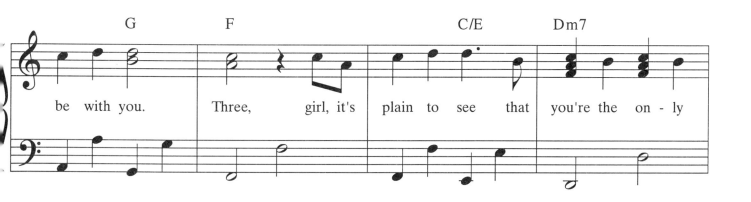

be with you. Three, girl, it's plain to see that you're the on - ly

Verse 2:
It's so incredible, the way things work themselves out.
And all emotional, once you know what it's all about, hey.
And undesirable, for us to be apart.
I never would have made it very far,
'Cause you know you've got the keys to my heart.
'Cause one, you're like a dream come true.

I Want It That Way

Recorded by Backstreet Boys

Words and Music by
MAX MARTIN and
ANDREAS CARLSSON
Arranged by Richard Bradley

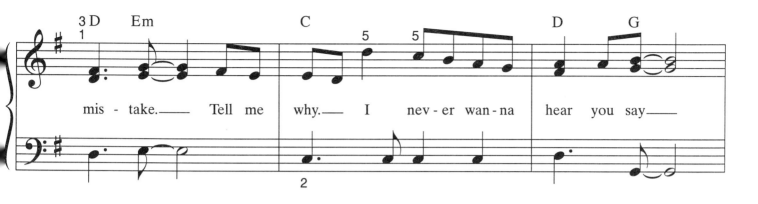

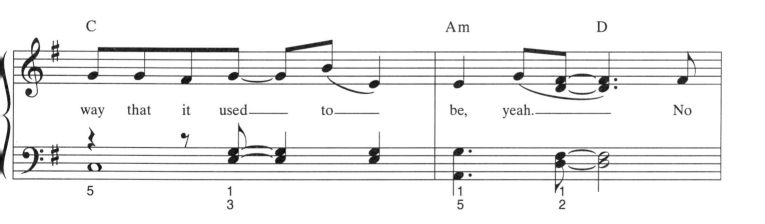

I Want It That Way - 4 - 2

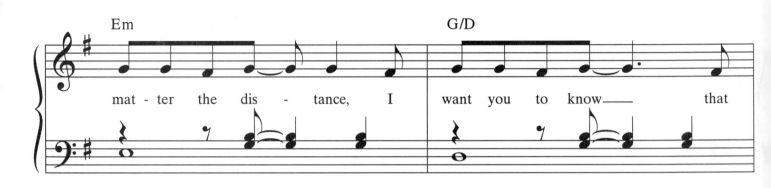

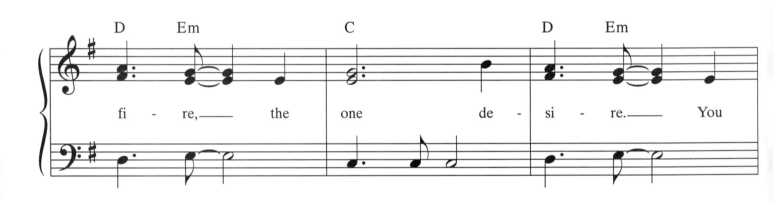

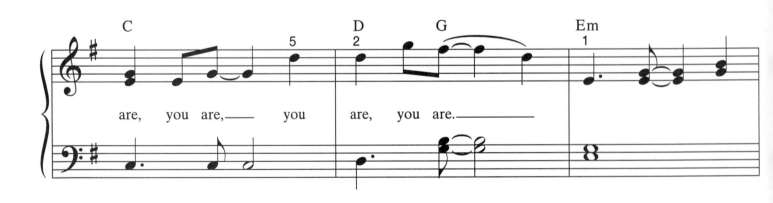

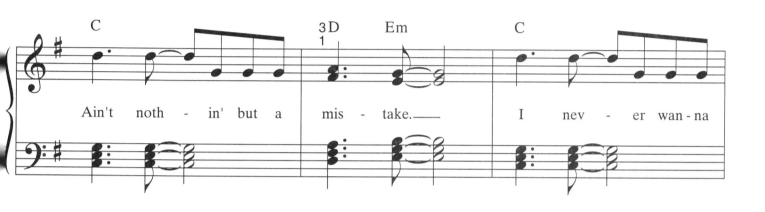

Verse 2:
But we are two worlds apart.
Can't reach to your heart
When you say
I want it that way.

Verse 3:
Am I your fire, your one desire?
Yes, I know it's too late,
But I want it that way.

I Want It That Way - 4 - 4

I Still Believe

Recorded by Mariah Carey

Words and Music by
ANTONINA ARMATO
and BEPPE CANTORELLI
Arranged by Richard Bradley

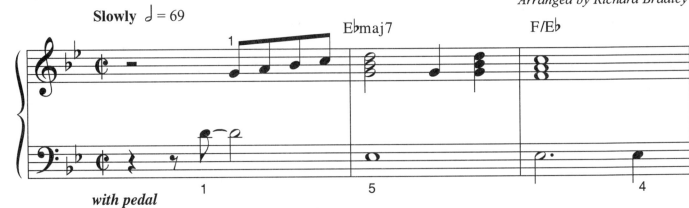

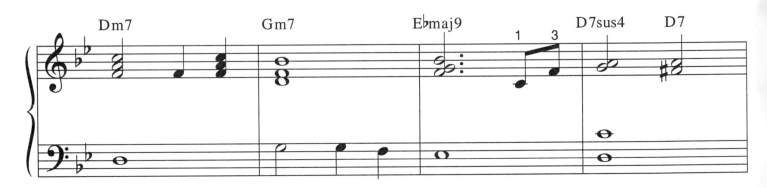

You look in my eyes and I

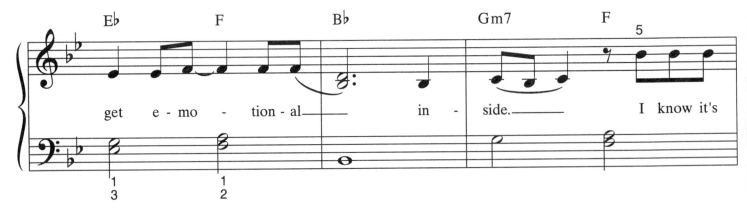

get e - mo - tion - al in - side. I know it's

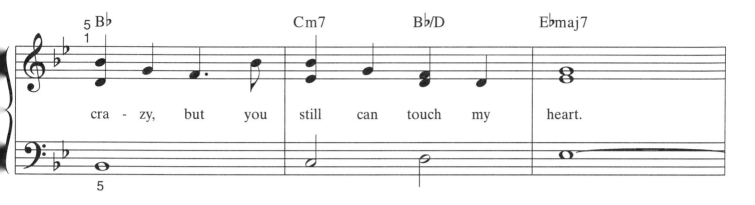

cra - zy, but you still can touch my heart.

And af - ter all this time,_____ you'd think that I_____

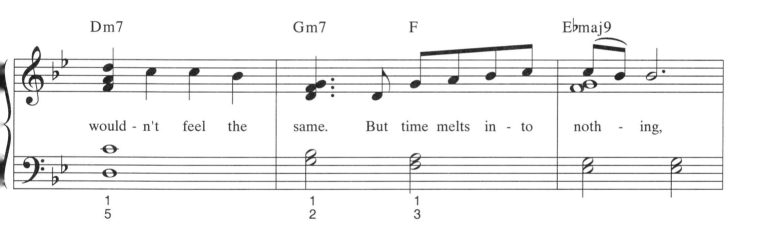

would - n't feel the same. But time melts in - to noth - ing,

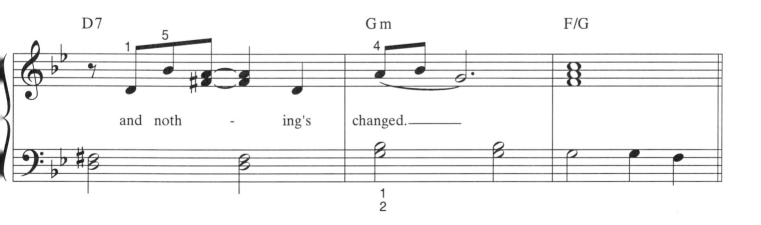

and noth - ing's changed._____

174

I Still Believe - 5 - 3

176

Verse 2:
Each day of my life, I'm filled with all the joy I could find.
You know that I am not the desperate type.
If there's one spark of hope left in my grasp,
I'll hold it with both hands.
It's worth the risk of burning to have a second chance.

Bye Bye Bye

Recorded by ★NSYNC

Words and Music by
KRISTIAN LUNDIN
JAKE and ANDREAS CARLSON
Arranged by Richard Bradley

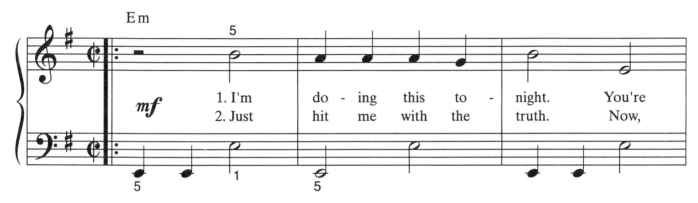

1. I'm do-ing this to-night. You're
2. Just hit me with the truth. Now,

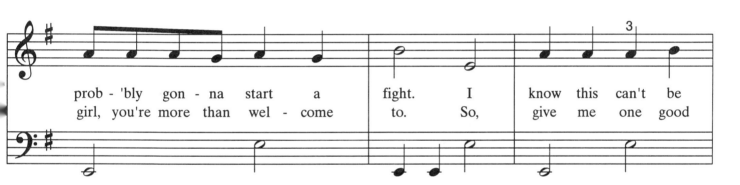

prob-'bly gon-na start a fight. I know this can't be
girl, you're more than wel-come to. So, give me one good

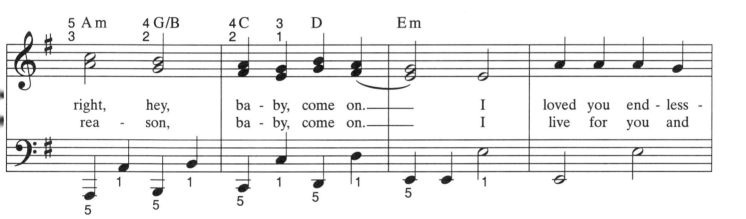

right, hey, ba-by, come on._____ I loved you end-less-
rea-son, ba-by, come on._____ I live for you and

ly, when you_____ were-n't there for me. So,
me and now I real-ly come to see that

Bye Bye Bye - 5 - 1

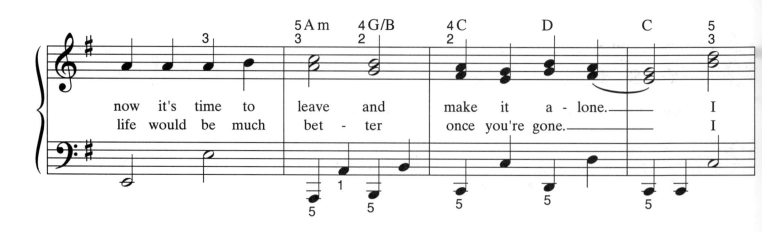

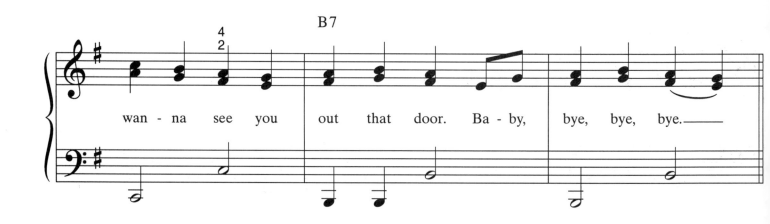

Bye Bye Bye - 5 - 3

ain't no lie. Ba-by, bye, bye, bye._

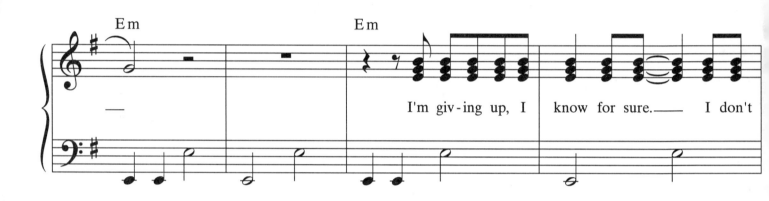

_ I'm giv-ing up, I know for sure._ I don't

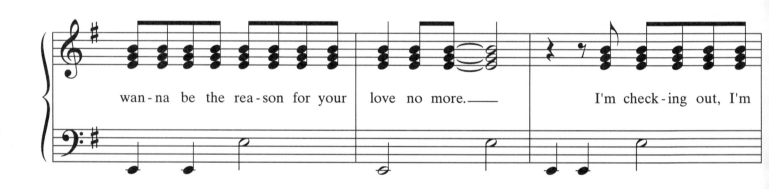

wan-na be the rea-son for your love no more._ I'm check-ing out, I'm

sign-ing off._ I don't wan-na be the los-er and I've had e-nough._

Bye Bye Bye - 5 - 5

Music of My Heart

From the Miramax Picture *Music of the Heart*
Recorded by Gloria Estefan and ★NSYNC

Words and Music by
DIANE WARREN
Arranged by Richard Bradley

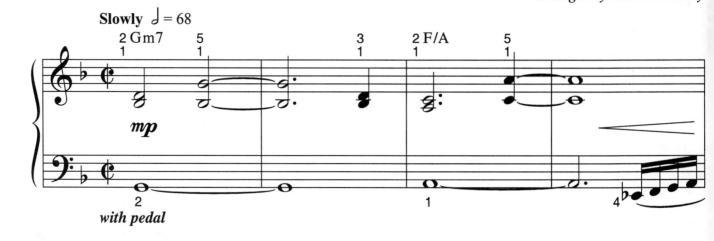

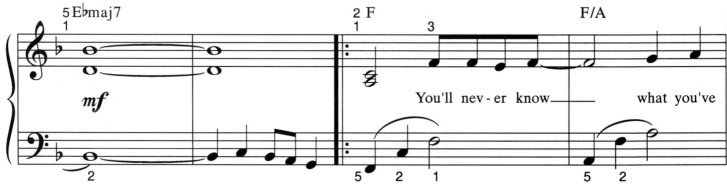

You'll nev - er know_____ what you've

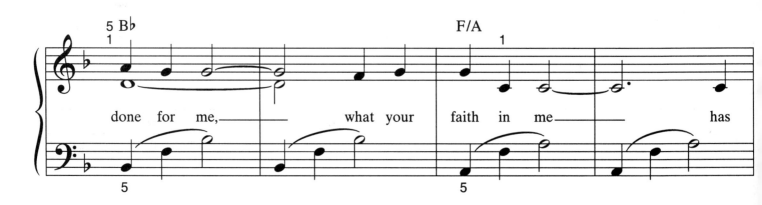

done for me,_____ what your faith in me_____ has

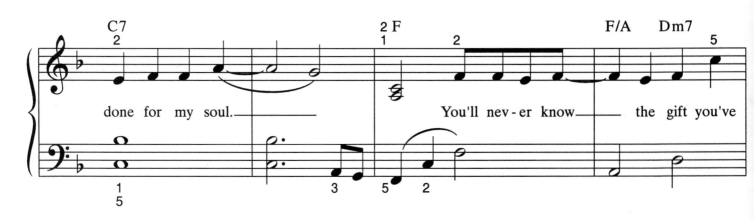

done for my soul._____ You'll nev - er know_____ the gift you've

Music of My Heart - 6 - 1

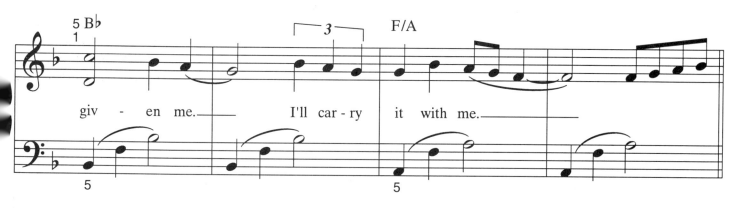

186

Music of My Heart - 6 - 5

Verse 2:
You were the one always on my side,
Always standing by, seeing me through.
You were the song that always made me sing.
I'm singing this for you.
Everywhere I go, I think of where I've been
And of the one who knew me better
Than anyone ever will again.

God Bless the U.S.A.

Recorded by Lee Greenwood

Words and Music by
LEE GREENWOOD
Arranged by Richard Bradley

God Bless the U.S.A. - 5 - 1

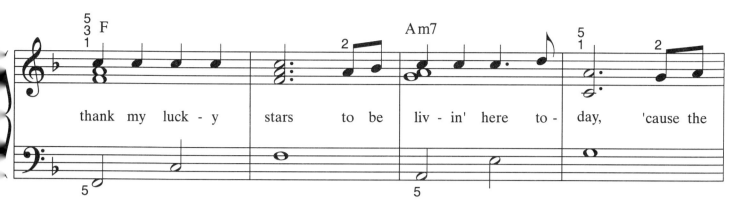

thank my luck - y stars to be liv - in' here to - day, 'cause the

flag still stands for free - dom and they can't take that a -

way. And I'm proud to be an A -

mer - i - can where at least I know I'm free. And I

won't for-get the   men who died, who   gave that right to

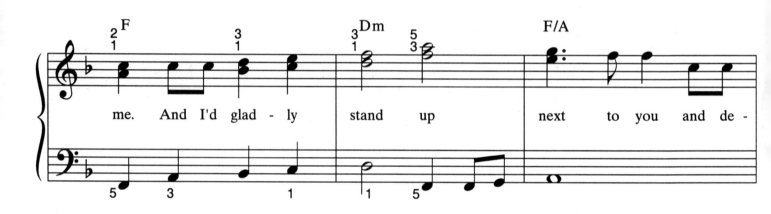

me.   And I'd glad-ly   stand   up   next   to you and de-

fend her still to- day,   'cause there ain't no doubt I   love this land,___

___   God   bless   the U.   S.   A.

Hous - ton and New York to L. A. well, there's

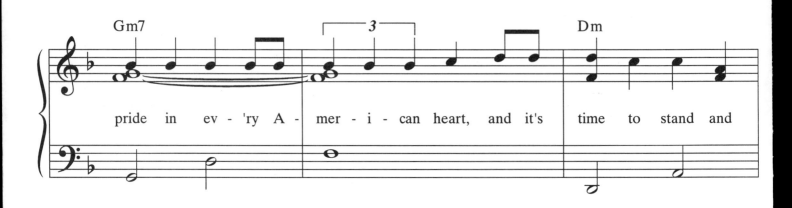

pride in ev - 'ry A - mer - i - can heart, and it's time to stand and

D.S. 𝄋 al Coda

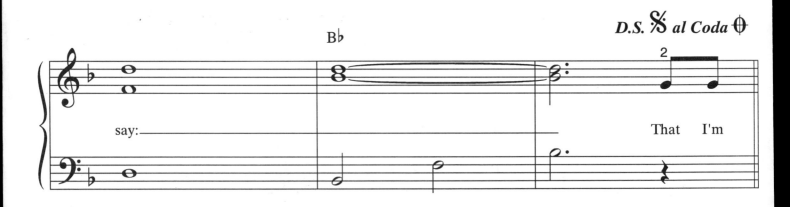

say: That I'm

Coda

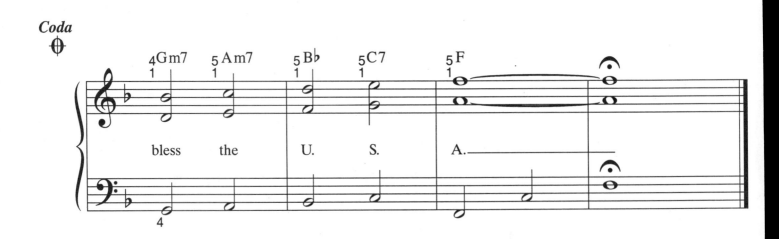

bless the U. S. A.